SCORE!

A Better Way to Do Busine$$: Moving from
Conflict to Collaboration

Ideas. Action. Impact.
**Wharton School
Publishing**

In the face of accelerating turbulence and change, business leaders and policy makers need new ways of thinking to sustain performance and growth.

Wharton School Publishing offers a trusted source for stimulating ideas from thought leaders who provide new mental models to address changes in strategy, management, and finance. We seek out authors from diverse disciplines with a profound understanding of change and its implications. We offer books and tools that help executives respond to the challenge of change.

Every book and management tool we publish meets quality standards set by The Wharton School of the University of Pennsylvania. Each title is reviewed by the Wharton School Publishing Editorial Board before being given Wharton's seal of approval. This ensures that Wharton publications are timely, relevant, important, conceptually sound or empirically based, and implementable.

To fit our readers' learning preferences, Wharton publications are available in multiple formats, including books, audio, and electronic.

To find out more about our books and management tools, visit us at whartonsp.com and Wharton's executive education site, exceed.wharton.upenn.edu.

SCORE!

A Better Way to Do Busine$$: Moving from Conflict to Collaboration

Thomas T. Stallkamp

Ideas. Action. Impact.
**Wharton School
Publishing**

Library of Congress Publication in Data: 2001115484

Publisher: *Tim Moore*
Executive Editor: *Jim Boyd*
Editorial Assistant: *Richard Winkler*
Development Editor: *Russ Hall*
Marketing Manager: *Martin Litkowski*
International Marketing Manager: *Tim Galligan*
Cover Designer: *Sandra Schroeder*
Managing Editor: *Gina Kanouse*
Senior Project Editor: *Kristy Hart*
Copy Editor: *Krista Hansing*
Indexer: *Angie Bess*
Interior Designer: *Meg VanArsdale*
Compositor: *Jake McFarland*
Manufacturing Buyer: *Dan Uhrig*

Ideas. Action. Impact.
Wharton School Publishing

© 2005 by Pearson Education, Inc.
Publishing as Wharton School Publishing
Upper Saddle River, New Jersey 07458

Wharton School Publishing offers excellent discounts on this book when ordered in quantity for bulk purchases or special sales. For more information, please contact U.S. Corporate and Government Sales, 1-800-382-3419, corpsales@pearsontechgroup.com. For sales outside the U.S., please contact International Sales at international@pearsoned.com.

Company and product names mentioned herein are the trademarks or registered trademarks of their respective owners.

Printed in the United States of America

First Printing, March 2005

ISBN 0-13-143526-4

Pearson Education LTD.
Pearson Education Australia PTY, Limited.
Pearson Education Singapore, Pte. Ltd.
Pearson Education North Asia, Ltd.
Pearson Education Canada, Ltd.
Pearson Educatión de Mexico, S.A. de C.V.
Pearson Education—Japan
Pearson Education Malaysia, Pte. Ltd.

Ideas. Action. Impact.
Wharton School Publishing

Bernard Baumohl
THE SECRETS OF ECONOMIC INDICATORS
Hidden Clues to Future Economic Trends and Investment Opportunities

Sayan Chatterjee
FAILSAFE STRATEGIES
Profit and Grow from Risks That Others Avoid

Sunil Gupta, Donald R. Lehmann
MANAGING CUSTOMERS AS INVESTMENTS
The Strategic Value of Customers in the Long Run

Stuart L. Hart
CAPITALISM AT THE CROSSROADS
The Unlimited Business Opportunities in Solving the World's Most Difficult Problems

Lawrence G. Hrebiniak
MAKING STRATEGY WORK
Leading Effective Execution and Change

Robert Mittelstaedt
WILL YOUR NEXT MISTAKE BE FATAL?
Avoiding the Chain of Mistakes That Can Destroy Your Organization

Mukul Pandya, Robbie Shell, Susan Warner, Sandeep Junnarkar, Jeffrey Brown
NIGHTLY BUSINESS REPORT PRESENTS LASTING LEADERSHIP
What You Can Learn from the Top 25 Business People of Our Times

C. K. Prahalad
THE FORTUNE AT THE BOTTOM OF THE PYRAMID
Eradicating Poverty Through Profits

Scott A. Shane
FINDING FERTILE GROUND
Identifying Extraordinary Opportunities for New Ventures

Oded Shenkar
THE CHINESE CENTURY
The Rising Chinese Economy and Its Impact on the Global Economy, the Balance of Power, and Your Job

Yoram (Jerry)Wind, Colin Crook, with Robert Gunther
THE POWER OF IMPOSSIBLE THINKING
Transform the Business of Your Life and the Life of Your Business

To the Chrysler team that implemented SCORE and to my best friends who continue to encourage me to try to change the system.

Contents

10 The Conversion Experience 169

11 Breaking the Mold: Moving to Collaboration 187

Appendix 207

Index 219

Acknowledgments

Quite a bit of time has passed from when the idea of this book was first presented until it was finally completed. During that time, I consulted with numerous business friends, acquaintances, and colleagues who encouraged me to present the story of how the business climate in which we operate could be improved. The experience of living in the ups and downs of the automotive business for over 30 years gave me access to many people with colorful stories (sometimes too colorful to be printed), great ideas, and fascinating insights into what is wrong and what needs to be fixed.

The first group to thank is the employees of the former Chrysler Corporation who helped turn what began as a unique concept into a functioning program that was the envy of the industry. Of particular importance are the past and present members of

Chrysler's Procurement and Supply activity who made it actually exciting and fun as we worked jointly with suppliers to revive the company and to create a truly great enterprise. Among those who helped lead the change were Peter Rosenfeld, Barry Price, Steve Zimmer, Bernie Bedard, all of whom were part of a great team. Additionally, the team of fellow Chrysler officers that embraced the idea and joined to bring it to life: Francois Castaing, Denny Pawley, and Tom Gale. None of our efforts could have been successful without the leadership, support and humor of Bob Lutz, who helped tear down the old structure and ideas. His personal encouragement of the SCORE program was a primary reason we have a story to tell.

The second group is the leaders in the supplier community around the globe who responded to our request for collaboration and cost-reduction ideas. They were the group that produced the actual results that fueled the engine to establish the Extended Enterprise®*. Some of the early leaders were Sam Gabria of Goodyear; Don Walker of Magna; Shinji Yazaki of Yazaki Corp; Dave Nelson now at Delphi; C. Ujie of Denso; the late Gene Richter of IBM; and all the other great executives who kept telling us that we were on the right track. They showed that communication and common purpose could build lasting relationships between companies.

Another invaluable group of support was the faculty and administration at the universities that helped highlight the organization changes we were making in our industry. Teaching and working with the students and faculty of Georgetown University, Miami University, and Babson College brought insights and helped focus the ideas that are presented in this book. The interest and enthusiasm shown by our graduate classes helped expand the concept into a broader industrial management application.

* Extended Enterprise® is a Registered Trademark of DaimlerChrysler Corporation.

I particularly want to thank Jon Maples, now at Visteon, for his assistance, ideas, and help in implementing the programs outlined here while we worked together at Chrysler. While many people supported the initial idea, Jon's focus on measurement, process, and open communication were responsible for the growth of the collaboration program. I was fortunate to have him to bounce ideas off and to bring his considerable intellectual abilities into real practice.

Writing a book for the first time by oneself is often a frustrating and exasperating experience. Several people helped me get through the process, especially: Jim Boyd, my editor at Wharton School Publishing who pushed and guided me all the way; Carrie Geeck, my administrative assistant, who typed and retyped endless drafts without complaint; Bruce Wagner, recently of MSX for his valuable counsel; and Joel Shulman, at Babson's Blank Center for Entrepreneurship who first introduced me to the publisher.

Finally, the most important group of my long-time friends and family, led by my wife, Ann, and sons, Tim and Greg, who were always supportive and encouraging as they lived this journey every day. All of you have had to put up with listening to the stories and problems for far too long. Now maybe we can help make some positive changes occur in the business world.

About the Author

Thomas T. Stallkamp is the founder and principal of Collaborative Management, LLC, a private consulting firm that specializes in implementing changes to business practices. He is also an industrial partner at Ripplewood Holdings, LLC, a private equity firm in New York.

Before he founded Collaborative Management, Stallkamp was CEO and chairman of MSX International, a global provider of collaborative enterprise services. Previously, Stallkamp was vice chairman of DaimlerChrysler Corporation. He also served as its president and a member of its board of management. During almost 20 years at Chrysler Corporation, he helped lead the company to new stability and growth in the uncommonly competitive automotive industry. During his tenure as president, Chrysler was the most profitable company in the auto industry.

Stallkamp became known for developing new business processes and enhanced partnerships with the automotive supply community, thereby improving product quality and cost efficiencies. He pioneered the development of a unique partnership approach to corporate supplier relations under Chrysler's Extended Enterprise® concept.

He serves on the boards of Visteon Corporation, Baxter International, and MSX International. He is also on the Board of Trustees of Babson College, where he is also an adjunct professor in its Graduate Entrepreneurship Center.

Stallkamp holds a Bachelor's degree in industrial management and economics, and a Master's degree in business administration from Miami University (Ohio); he received honorary doctorates from Georgetown University and Miami University. He resides with his wife in Birmingham, Michigan, and has two grown sons.

INTRODUCTION

The first three years into the twenty-first century have not been a high-water mark for American business management. Both businessmen and the general public have suffered through accounting scandals, management malfeasance, and blatant greed that make the actions of the old robber barons look tame. Governmental legislation and regulation have been enacted to restore the public confidence in business managers and to protect private investors. This turmoil and the resultant backlash of reform can be viewed as a cycle that will correct itself and permit business to resume as normal. But what if it doesn't?

In the summer of 2001, I gave a speech to a gathering of automotive executives, entitled "Fixing a Broken Economic Model—A Case for Supplier Alliances." In it, I suggested that the way the automotive industry dealt with its suppliers, dealers, and employees at that time had become too adversarial and that changes should be adopted before we ran out of time to react. The reaction was predictable: lots of agreement from the supply base and rejection from the automakers. I even got called into one of the Big Three automakers and asked to explain why I was fermenting such heresy. That told me I had struck a nerve.

This book contends that the basic business model that has developed over the last century might be broken and that, instead of reverting to "normal" practices and methods, we should consider a new model. The present model is based on the strong independence and separation of firms from other companies, which makes collaboration or alliances hard to propose and even harder to implement. This model forces companies to take adversarial positions when dealing with other firms and drives the merger activity that is prevalent even in today's economy.

This book is built on the premise that companies—and, more important, their managers—can adopt more collaborative and strategic partnerships with related firms, to help the economy maximize its growth into the future. Situations have changed in the last few years beyond the accounting and management scandals, requiring modern managers to adopt a new model based on relationships, measurement of goals, and common strategies. Capital continues to be limited even in periods of low interest rates, as banking institutions try to limit their exposure to risky industries. Global competition threatens our existing American business model by opening our own markets to new, more entrepreneurial firms from cultures that operate much differently than ours. As these firms enter our own market and establish a new presence, we cannot be sure that they will operate completely under the American form that has been so strong in the last century.

Although people have been talking and preaching about ways to increase collaborations for years, only a few successful examples have arisen. During my 20 years at the Chrysler Corporation, and through the merger of DaimlerChrysler, we developed a different management approach to dealing with our external suppliers and our own employees. Using the principles under Chrysler's Extended Enterprise concept, we were able to put collaboration into practice in the 1990s and prove that it could be more than a soft philosophical idea. During that period, we proved that closer and more strategic approaches to suppliers, employees, and other constituents could raise the level of corporate performance and financial results. Many other advanced companies, including Dell Computer and Intel, are now using the principles that we helped create. Even such old-line managements as the U.S. Air Force are exploring them. These principles are more difficult to use than the old-line command and control approach that is still the prevalent style, but strategic and planned collaboration is spreading rapidly.

If American business is to continue to thrive in the twenty-first century, as it did in the twentieth, we must make radical changes in how we run and manage our institutions. The current approach forces a separation of companies and legally insists on dealing at arm's length. This might be good for ensuring competition, but with its negative slant against close cooperation, it could be the reason we have seen some of the bizarre and massive moves to acquire or merge with other firms for growth. The well-intentioned changes that Congress and regulators are forcing onto business and management might be only Band-Aids that mask deeper issues. As we all try to rebuild confidence in American business, we should try to move forward instead of just patching up our wounds and regrouping to fight the same old fight.

I started this work to describe how companies can improve their financial performance by changing the way they approach their supply chain. But after more than 30 years in management positions at extremely large corporations, I now realize that we have to change our whole approach to management, with both our employees and our suppliers. That change must start at the very top of the organization and be thought through in detail to see how it impacts the existing corporate culture. Many of the examples and stories used in this book come from manufacturing or industrial settings, but the problems that adversarial management practices create impact all businesses, including those in the service and financial sectors. Little is unique across our management practices in America, and the idea of forming closer alliances affects any firm.

A word of caution is required to those of us who graduated with traditional MBA degrees: Our training and the way we have been practicing business over the years has instilled in us a great deal of cynicism and doubt toward any change in the way we practice management. The following chapters outline what is wrong with the current system that has served so well in the past, and present a new approach that, on the surface, violates some of the principles under which we now operate. Reflecting on the way it works now, on the difficulty communicating across people and firms, and on the long-standing after-effects of adversarial management will help you understand that the changes being recommended are possible, practical, and necessary. The chapters include ways to monitor, measure, and track how the new system is working, to hold bean counters and financial analysts at bay. When the macro results come in, the whole organization will become believers and realize that change is necessary.

I believe that, with its vastly increased global competition and the baggage of historical organizational thinking, the next few decades of the twenty-first century will be a laboratory for change that we must explore. The old ways of the past that centered on a command and control style of management are about to be blown away by a younger, more international, less loyal, and less tolerant workforce. This book is about finding a way to end the current adversarial tone of management. I hope that it can create change, not just discussion. Reactions to speeches that I have given to major industry audiences on this subject have encouraged me to go beyond the obvious scope of supply chain management and offer up a wholesale change in general management. Applied correctly, with significant planning, it can improve the culture of a firm and stimulate growth so that the next generation thinks it is rewarding to go into a business career.

1

BREAKING THE MOLD

There Has to Be a Better Way

All the powers of management at the Chrysler Corporation were
seated in the massive leather chairs of the Executive Conference
Room[1] on that still morning in 1990. The senior operating and
administrative members of the company sat around the oval table,
while various staff members eager to watch the show from safe
positions (the peanut gallery, in company jargon) sat in chairs
along the walls. At the head of the table was Bob Lutz, then president of Chrysler, who used this weekly meeting of his staff and
others to review the operational and financial issues affecting the

company in the short run. In short, this meeting was intended to cajole the functional areas under his command to update and inform each other on what was happening in their respective areas, even though information sharing was not an item that the Chrysler culture had previously encouraged. Lutz had arrived at Chrysler several years earlier from Ford, where he had been well schooled in the politics of command and control. At Chrysler, Lutz used his energy and personal enthusiasm to break down the silos of the separate functions and was beginning to build the team with which he would run the company successfully for the next eight years.

Jim Donlon, the corporate controller, who was not a part of the regular operating team but occasionally attended the meetings as an observer, had something urgent to say today. He rose from his seat in the hush to announce that the competition had launched a deadly new cost-reduction program that required an immediate response to keep Chrysler from losing ground.

It was a time of severely depressed demand and profitability for the "Big Three" manufacturers in the domestic auto industry, and Chrysler was perennially the weakest and most threatened of the bunch. The sit-up-in-your-chair heart of Donlon's report was that Ford was rumored to be implementing a forced mandatory price-reduction action on all its suppliers. The auto industry in Detroit is closely knit and the supply base members (and executive teams) were constantly comparing notes among themselves, so there were few secrets in town. Certainly, an action as drastic as this one could not be kept quiet for long.

Ford had electronically modified all its existing production purchase orders with its thousands of suppliers to pay only 95 percent of what had been previously negotiated with them. All invoices that the suppliers sent were factored to 95 percent of their value, and Ford sent the reduced amount as full payment. This action was both unorthodox and highly effective. Instead of having to negotiate with each of the thousands of suppliers and arrive at a potentially different answer with each, this mechanical method merely changed the prices at the push of a button, saving Ford millions in purchases. It also severely upset the supply base members. Because they were extremely fragmented and separate, they had no ability to resist as a collective group. Each firm was left to individually decide either to resist by not shipping and risk losing all revenue instantly, or to continue to ship and accept the new terms. The action was unpopular and created major issues in the press. But Ford used its own financial crisis to justify the action.

The Chrysler finance team's suggestion was that the company should take similar action immediately because the automotive supply base was very common across the Big Three manufacturers. If the supply base members conceded to the Ford action, Chrysler and GM would be at a competitive disadvantage unless they took similar actions.

At the time, I was heading up procurement and supply, as executive vice president at Chrysler. I took the floor and expressed the opinion that, although the Ford action was effective in the short term from their position, it would create more tension with the supply base in an already difficult atmosphere. It was unexpected in its timing, but not from its source; Ford had traditionally ranked low in surveys from suppliers for collaborative policies. Many of us had come from Ford to Chrysler during the dark days of the 1980 Federal Loan Guarantee Program, and we were familiar with the culture and attitude there that could produce such an unpopular and arbitrary action. I felt that if Chrysler were to follow, we would be endorsing a policy that seemed completely against the unique one we had been trying to build.

Fortunately, Lutz sided that day with my recommendation to break out on a different path, and we refused to follow Ford's action. We responded with a unique system built on mutual negotiation and shared savings that became a decade-long program at Chrysler. Known as the Extended Enterprise®, it became a unique way to reduce costs and improve supplier relations at the same time. But on that day in 1990, it would be an understatement to say we had a few disbelievers in the finance office who wanted us to take the same short-term action that Ford had done to boost our earnings. The program we developed worked, though, and showed not only Chrysler, but also the rest of the industry, that following what appear to be industry trends doesn't always produce the best answer.

This book analyzes the predominant way business managers handle relationships with other companies in their daily operation. It is almost impossible to find a company of any size that can exist solely by itself. Our economy operates in a web of related actions. You will see how the manner in which companies deal with these important interrelationships is not always logical and that there are many different approaches. It becomes a question of whether to stay the course and take predictable and accepted actions, or to try something different. Often it also involves the struggle for control and domination that has come to characterize many business dealings.

The Clash of Opposite Approaches

One of the best contrasts in styles and tactics in relationship management and their results occurred in Detroit in the last decade of the twentieth century. In 1992, Jack Smith, then chairman of

General Motors, brought over to the United States a Spanish cost expert he found within the company when he was in charge of GM Europe. Smith thought the unusual but apparently effective techniques that J. Ignacio Lopez wielded in Europe would be just the thing to turn around the rising costs of the larger enterprise of GM in the United States. Lopez arrived in Detroit in May of that year as a relatively unknown entity who immediately made a name for himself as the executive vice president of purchasing.

Lopez exhibited a confident and somewhat colorful personality as he entered a town that had learned long ago how the "game" of manufacturer/supplier relations was played. Lopez took pride in several unusual personal habits, such as wearing his watch on the opposite arm and following a strict "warrior" diet that required eating a rigid regimen of health foods seven times a day. He immediately set out to challenge the existing commercial system by banning GM employees from going to business lunches with suppliers, and he attacked the company's cost structures with a vengeance. His early success was considerable, in both his impact on the industry and his initial results to lower GM's prices.

The techniques that Lopez used were demanding and arbitrary. If suppliers would not agree to immediate price reductions, their contract was terminated and given to another lower-priced source. Existing multiyear contracts that had just been negotiated before his arrival were ripped up and substituted by aggressive market testing. One of Lopez's more flagrant actions was shipping proprietary drawings on patented items to offshore manufacturers with limited technology, to get a cheaper price. These lower-overhead quotes were then used to force the inventing firm into lowering its prices, or risk losing the business. Suppliers were forced to decide whether to continue with GM on the automaker's terms or to sever the relationship.

The supplier community reacted with both panic and anger. With his aggressive tactics, the new guy from Spain had changed the rules of the game that had been in play for decades. While they complained and griped, Lopez forced and coerced his suppliers into submission. Resistance to the strong-arm tactics often meant that parts were resourced to new companies offering lower costs to get into the GM "family." The opportunity to move into favored status with the largest automaker on the planet was too strong for many to resist. Long-established relationships were suddenly replaced with newly formed alliances with sources that sometimes were making a particular part for the first time.

The mission was too much for one man to accomplish single-handedly, so Lopez brought over a crew of disciples who had worked with him in Europe and who were familiar with his aggressive tactics. They were put in charge of the various departments and spread the warrior approach throughout the company. In just nine months, during 1992 and early 1993, Lopez transformed GM purchasing into an aggressive machine whose actions and tactics were often both brutal and arbitrary. But he produced results, and GM management never bothered to ask how he achieved them. Much later, when asked if he ever reflected on how Lopez was achieving such apparent success while working for him in Europe, Bob Eaton, who, as Smith's successor as chairman of GM Europe, had promoted Lopez to a vice president position, replied, "I never bothered to ask how he got the results he did; I just counted them up." Apparently, the end justified the means to him and his company.

Lopez did achieve results—or, at least, the financial community thought so. Merrill Lynch reported that he produced $300 million in savings in the fourth quarter of 1992. The story has a much more interesting ending, as discussed later, but as 1993 rolled around, Lopez and his adversarial role were the talk of Detroit, if not the automotive world. Coming on the heels of Chrysler's brush with financial troubles, the stage was set for a live experiment pitting two completely different approaches against each other.

A Completely Different Approach

I came into the job of running Chrysler's procurement and supply activity in 1990. After spending a career of almost two decades watching and participating in the harsh world of automotive procurement, I had decided it was time to try something different in management techniques. By the time 1992 arrived, the Chrysler Corporation was in full swing with its unique and different approach to managing suppliers. As mentioned earlier, Bob Lutz had given full corporate support to adopting a system utilizing the suppliers as partners with Chrysler in both production and development—that is, a collaborative approach to dealing with its supply base. Using a detailed proprietary goal and measurement system labeled SCORE, for Supplier Cost Reduction Effort, the company was wringing costs out of its system by soliciting and approving supplier ideas to change the old operating system. Suppliers were asked to outline ways in which doing business with Chrysler was creating costs in either their systems or Chrysler's systems. Instead of mandating reductions or price decreases, Chrysler offered to work with the supply base to implement submitted ideas that streamlined the business or eliminated redundant efforts and costs.

Although it took some time to get started, by 1992, the SCORE approach had been incorporated into a supply-management philosophy called the Extended Enterprise. The concept was to treat suppliers and dealers as independent extensions of the firm. Because their destiny and fortunes were directly linked to Chrysler's, the idea was to build a virtual team atmosphere in which all parties focused on reducing the cost of developing and producing vehicles. The constructive supply-side suggestions worked to reduce both the supplier's costs and those at Chrysler. There were no firm rules for submitting the ideas, and no area of the company was off-limits to outside ideas. An essential element was that the savings that resulted from these ideas were voluntary and up to the supplier to define and contribute. Chrysler did not dictate the amount nor the manner that savings were to be achieved. Instead, they turned the situation around and asked the suppliers to identify ways that they could reduce their costs in doing business through their own eyes, rather than from Chrysler's view. This was previously unheard of in an industry where the Big Three always dominated the control.

Chrysler encouraged its suppliers to contribute most of the savings in the way of price reductions, but it also encouraged them to keep some of them, to reinforce their profit margins and redirect it into their own businesses. This concept of sharing the savings with the suppliers was truly unique, and the supply base members quickly supported it. A relatively simple data system recorded and monitored the savings.

The approach required close cooperation among all areas of the company, especially procurement and engineering. These two normally separate departments jointly developed and shared the cost-reduction targets for SCORE. Weekly reports followed the submission of supplier ideas and were tracked to the appropriate internal area that would approve the suggestion. This prevented ideas from languishing in the system, as had previous attempts to solicit ideas from the supply base. This internal follow-up removed the skepticism that initially greeted the program. Chrysler's internal communications highlighted measurements of how suppliers were performing, and the mainstream media publicized the success stories, to help spread the word that this alternative program was working. The auto industry is a very close community, and word quickly spread about how the Extended Enterprise was working.

The Extended Enterprise concept also relied on the assumption that the business relationship would continue over time. Chrysler promoted the idea that as long as cost, quality, delivery, and technology targets were met, the business relationship would be preserved and not resourced. Instead of using traditional resourcing, if a problem in one of these areas occurred at Chrysler, the supplier was given a chance to correct it before an alternative supplier was introduced. Resourcing is a common practice in purchasing, in which an existing contract is terminated, and the production and revenue are moved to a new supplier.

The Chrysler system was in operation when Lopez arrived on the scene in Detroit. Although the Chrysler system had produced some significant initial savings that totaled more than $500 million in cumulative costs by mid-1992, some skeptics thought that this was low-hanging fruit and questioned whether it could be sustained. Many industry reporters and analysts waited to see if we could honor and hold to our promise of sharing the savings and respecting long-term commitments. The fortunes of Chrysler began to improve during this time because of both the cost reductions that SCORE and the Extended Enterprise produced, and the expanding volumes of minivans and sport utility vehicles. To continue its progress, Chrysler needed to accelerate its programs. The arrival of the Spaniard with a different approach at General Motors turned out to provide that acceleration.

Business Gravitates to the Easiest Relationship

The fury and turmoil that Lopez's actions at General Motors created played into the hands of Chrysler. We never considered Lopez a threat or an enemy, but the press quickly turned our two vastly different approaches into a personal battle. This was helped along by the business press, but even more by suppliers who had previously been skeptical of the Extended Enterprise. They needed to be shown that companies could be trusted because the system in which they had operated for so long played on mistrust and suspicion. Chrysler had begun to build a different order of doing things, but it was so contrary to the existing norm in the industry that it took another push to convince the doubters. GM and Lopez provided that additional emphasis.

As General Motors turned up the heat on its suppliers for more price concessions, the general climate became much more supportive of what we were trying to do at Chrysler. The supply bases were very similar between the two companies, as they are in any industry, be it aerospace, retail, or financial services. Suppliers in a given industry tend to isolate themselves to that industry because of common products and services and lower overall cost. Most industry analysts estimate that the amount of common suppliers in the domestic auto industry in the 1990s was 80 to 90 percent, meaning that the same supplier would provide similar parts to each of the Big Three automakers. Gone were the days when each company built its own loyal supporting cast of suppliers. The efficiencies of spreading costs over all three major manufacturers resulted in a very concentrated industry.

The aggressive and controversial actions of GM drove suppliers to look more closely at the more collaborative model being promoted at Chrysler. The comparisons were obvious. The GM model was arbitrary and dictatorial, and it placed the supplier at a disadvantage by always threatening to resource the business if a lower-cost manufacturer were found elsewhere. Chrysler's model was collaborative, based on shared savings, and it encouraged the suppliers to be in charge of their own businesses. The comparisons between the two systems were dramatic, and these helped fuel the controversy in Detroit over which system could produce the largest and most lasting results.

The Big Three purchasing executives had been meeting for several years before Lopez arrived to discuss common ways to improve the industry in areas such as communications, quality initiatives, and other nonproprietary or competitive areas. One of these common areas involved a survey of the supply base members to determine the relative differences in suppliers' perception of the automakers. A consulting firm of university professors was hired to quantify the differences between the Big Three manufacturers and the rest of the recent transplanted companies. After much negotiation, the Big Three purchasing departments all agreed to use this independent group to survey the common supply base. They developed a statistically valid survey to be sent to thousands of people who dealt with the original equipment manufacturers (OEMs). The three companies funded the survey, and each was allowed its own separate questions, although there were approximately 14 common questions on such things as trust factors, level of engagement, arbitrary cost pressures, and similar business issues.

The results of the study[2] confirmed what Chrysler believed. Relationships do matter, and there was a wide variance among the three Detroit manufacturers. It showed that there were large differences in the ways the domestic manufacturers approached their suppliers from the ways used by the newly arrived foreign-owned OEMs. The main difference was in the positive manner in which the foreign transplants established an atmosphere of trust and close cooperation with their suppliers.

Figure 1.1 shows the results for the critical category of supplier trust versus the benchmark in the industry, Toyota. While the Chrysler program was in effect, Chrysler consistently equaled Toyota. Only after the merger with Daimler-Benz in 1998 did it begin to fall as the emphasis became more traditional.

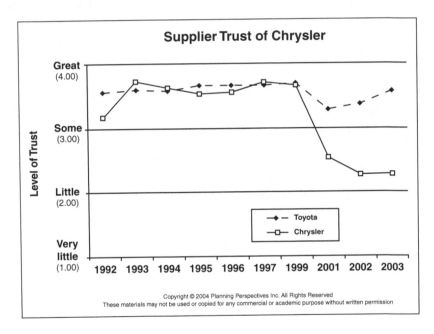

Figure 1.1—Supplier Trust of Chrysler

Although the domestic manufacturers continued to rank lower than the foreign transplants, Chrysler scored significantly higher than General Motors in such areas as trust, fairness in relationships, ability to generate cost savings, and ability to build relationships. Chrysler believed this survey accurately reflected the attitude in the industry and validated that the company was on the right track for changing the system.

The Final Chapter of Lopez

The final chapter in this controversial clash of philosophies came only nine months after Lopez arrived in the United States. Having generated much attention with his tactics, which were directly opposite to those of Chrysler, Lopez created one of the most bizarre chapters in American business. On March 13, 1993, Volkswagen ended a week of rumor and announced that it had hired Lopez away from General Motors and had offered him a seat on its management board as head of production and procurement. The story shocked both Jack Smith and the rest of the GM management, who had become impressed with his results of cost improvements. They quickly responded and announced on March 15 that they had persuaded Lopez to remain at GM by giving him more authority over production. GM scheduled a press conference for the following morning, at which Chairman Smith was to announce the retention and enlarged responsibility for Lopez. Instead, just one half-hour before the press briefing, Smith was forced to announce that his deal had fallen apart and confirmed that Lopez had again changed his mind and was indeed defecting to VW. The way the story unfolded, and the shock of the final resolution, further convinced the suppliers that trust and loyalty were not in the vocabulary of the once famous—now infamous—cost-cutter.

In a final twist, a short time later, General Motors announced that it was filing legal actions, including charges of criminal theft, against Lopez for stealing proprietary corporate documents and cost information that he took with him to VW. The case was pressed in federal court but was dropped several years later after

Lopez was critically injured and suffered permanent brain damage in an auto accident in Spain. At the time of Lopez's defection, though, GM moved to address the complaints of the suppliers and industry analysts by naming Richard Wagner, a young, personable, and rising financial executive, to replace Lopez, as a sign that the company needed to modify its adversarial approach. Wagner later replaced Smith as the CEO and chairman of General Motors.

Comparing the Two Approaches

On the surface, the GM/Lopez approach might not appear that different from the Chrysler Extended Enterprise approach in the results achieved. Both were cost-reduction programs, and both served their initial purposes in the short run because both companies reduced their cost base. But the differences are much more than just style and approach. The arbitrary nature of Lopez's demands created deep-seated animosity within the General Motors supply community that impacted their development of new products. Although some current prices were reduced, suppliers began to talk about turning down future contracts because their profitability was in question. Lopez's successor quickly moved to rebuild the element of trust, to avoid widespread defection from General Motors. More than 25 percent of the parts being procured had been resourced to new suppliers under Lopez in the short period of nine months he had been in power. Industry and financial analysts have cited this action as one of the reasons GM's quality deteriorated during this period. This resourcing created turmoil and dislocation in a system that was already fragile from a quality standpoint.

The Chrysler Extended Enterprise system encouraged continuity by having suppliers work toward defined targets on future programs as well as current ones. The targets for new models were based on market-driven prices supported by the projected selling price of the new vehicle. If a firm could meet those targets, it was awarded the business on a long-term basis. It could count on Chrysler not to arbitrarily change its mind and demand more concessions, as long as the objectives were met. In this manner, the stability of the commercial relationship was more secure. Stability meant less need for protection actions, such as front-loaded profits. If the contract was long term and the customer was predictable and reliable, the supplier's profits could be more evenly spread over the period. Suppliers viewed the Chrysler business as a better place to invest their limited development money.

Chrysler began to enjoy greater investment in new products because of the stable and defined relationships promoted there. Chrysler was able to introduce more new models faster using less of its own capital because suppliers were more inclined to bet on their futures. As previously mentioned, this then led to business relationships founded on predictability and fairness.

In a way, it was fortunate for General Motors that Lopez defected back to Europe when he did. If he had been permitted to continue, the animosity his approach created might have led to a major dislocation in supply at GM. There is a place where the short term meets the long term, and Lopez was on his way to destroying both with his unique relationship-management style.

A Call for Change

Clearly, the Lopez saga and the open clash between General Motors' and Chrysler Corporation's strategies is one of the most bizarre stories in the history of the largest industry in the world. It also highlights a real example of the differences between the two approaches to commerce, adversarial and collaborative.

Although this example deals with a specific industry, adversarial tactics and approaches dominate many other industries in American business. It is not limited just to the automotive industry, but it permeates such widely diverse industries as financial services, retail, and entertainment. In many ways, it seems to have become the standard way of managing commerce in this country.

The following chapters of this book challenge the existing commercial system and offer an alternative to the way many firms conduct business. Although the current system clearly works, it contains inefficiencies and does not get the most out of business relationships. As the global economy becomes much more competitive, the advantages of the American system are being reduced. Our labor costs continue to rise faster than in other countries. Our speed to market is hampered by having to communicate through a system that discourages open and shared development. Our industrial production in the United States is threatened as many industries mature and enter a declining phase, as witnessed by our automobile, steel, electronics, and apparel manufacturing.

Manufacturing is an essential element in any growing economy. The decline in the U.S. industrial base and the practice of lowering pay in service-sector jobs do not offer a happy outlook for the future of our country. We cannot become isolationist in our management practices, but we must look at the way we run our various businesses to see if we can adopt another approach. To regain our competitive advantage, American businesses must look at the way they operate and make substantial changes in the commercial system. Recent gains in productivity could be masking a problem that we are not creating enough jobs to maintain growth in employment over the long term. Increasing industrial production is one of the main ways for historic economic growth, and the declining production levels in this country send warning signs that we are running out of time to take action. This book outlines an alternative way that has worked in the past but that has not been widely embraced because it bucks the trend of commercial history and requires a different and difficult level of management interaction. But the situation facing our industrial manufacturing companies seems so severe that we must look at implementing some tough changes in the way we operate before the majority of our jobs go overseas and the United States becomes a service-dominated economy.

American businessmen like to think of themselves as action oriented and quick to make decisions. They now have in front of them a situation that requires some substantial changes instead of tweaks in the way we manage. It also requires a leap of faith in establishing trust between companies, just as humans do in the best personal relationships. Companies can make changes in attitude and direction to accomplish this transformation. What we have to do now is act before we run out of time and lose our industrial base forever. Time is clearly of the essence.

Endnotes

1. Some corporate facilities gnome who never was allowed into its lofty setting officially named the room Conference Room A, and the name stuck forever.

2. The study was performed by Planning Perspectives, Inc., initially for the Big Three OEMs separately. After 1995, it was performed jointly.

2

ADVERSARIAL COMMERCE AND WHY IT'S WRONG

Adversarial Commerce Defined

The behaviors Ford and General Motors exhibited (as discussed in the previous chapter) are examples of adversarial commerce. This term describes the negative and domineering manner many companies use to control their relationships in normal business dealings. Adversarial commerce is becoming increasingly common in the business world because it is based on using short-term leverage (such as Lopez's cost slashing at the expense of suppliers) from the value of the business to produce equally quick results. The major, or dominant, side is usually the manufacturer of the final product, such as an automobile or airplane manufacturer, or the provider of a service to the final customer, such as a financial institution or mass retailer. The minor, or submissive, side is a vendor of a necessary component or service, such as an automotive parts supplier or a grocery vendor. In these situations, the dominant side manages and controls the final production or distribution of the end product.

Under adversarial commerce, the dominant party applies economic leverage in a dictatorial, arbitrary manner. The company forces the subordinate party to concede to demands without considering the financial hardship or long-term effects those demands might create. This might seem to be a natural byproduct of size, responsibility, or power, but the negative aspect it creates colors the entire relationship. It forces even the adversarial firm to concentrate on the short-term results instead of building a sustainable and growing relationship. This battle for total control produces a situation not unlike that between a drug dealer and a user. Both need each other, but only one is in control of the situation. The drug dealer uses his access to the product to control the user, and the OEM uses his purchase contracts to control the supplier in much the same manner.

Adversarial commerce forces the two parties into a defensive posture that is counterproductive to building longer-term goals. Relationships based on distrust between two parties force them to protect their own profit position instead of work for joint solutions to joint problems. An underlying atmosphere of antagonism and defensiveness permeates the environment under this management style. Even though they are doing business together, the firms build barriers between each other, when they should be working more closely. Under adversarial commerce, companies use tactics that intentionally keep the relationship tense and unstable. The subsequent tendency is for both sides to seek maximum control over the other party and try to gain the most advantage.

From a practical standpoint, you might be tempted to question what is so wrong with companies using leverage to force suppliers into cooperation. Isn't this just the economic clout that we all expect a big firm to use? Many people might think that, in the Ford example, the company was quite crafty in implementing its forced price reductions. The answer is that, under adversarial commerce, there isn't any true cooperation. The short-term advantages that might be gained are swamped by the long-term harm and incremental costs built into a very protective commercial system. True, dictatorial methods might produce quick results. The issue is that, while producing these results, these methods generate longer-lasting negative responses that also add costs over the long term. Concentrating on the immediate results builds in a bias against collaboration.

The Practice Is Accelerating

The use of negative and dictatorial management practices is accelerating as economic conditions become more difficult and global competition increases. U.S. automakers (including the domestic Chrysler side of DaimlerChrysler) have all recently and uniformly resorted to very aggressive and arbitrary ways of dealing with their common suppliers. The immediate problem of their lack of profitability, created by high internal costs and poor product decisions, is straining their relationships with manufacturers. Until now, these manufacturers had depended upon the Big Three for the majority of their business. In doing so, they had assumed that a sense of loyalty existed with the OEM. The automotive press reports that relationships between the Big Three and their suppliers are at an all-time low compared to those of transplant or foreign manufacturers. The dominant manufacturers hide behind the excuse of hardship and the need to respond quickly to foreign competition. Instant price reductions and front-loaded cost "contributions" are reducing the collective profitability of the industry. The demands for immediate price reductions can come only out of the margins of suppliers, which further reduces the industry's ability to reinvest into the business.

Planning Perspectives, the same consulting company that performs the previously mentioned supplier surveys for the Big Three, emphasized the effects of this accelerating trend in their 2004 results:

> As a result of their respective handling of suppliers, there are some profound shifts going on in the industry that can't help but impact the U.S. Big Three's ability to compete going forward, said Henke [John Henke, president of Planning Perspectives, Inc., a firm that specializes in supplier relationships]. These changes are summarized in the following points:
>
> - Chrysler, Ford, and GM supplier working relations are falling behind Honda and Toyota at an increasing rate.
>
> - Suppliers are shifting resources (capital and R&D expenditures, service, and support) to Japanese Big Three, while reducing these for Domestic Big Three.

- Suppliers are increasing product quality at a greater rate for Japanese automakers, while merely maintaining quality levels for U.S. automakers.

- Supplier trust of Ford and General Motors has never been lower; conversely, trust for the Japanese OEMs has never been higher.

- Suppliers increasingly see the opportunity to make an acceptable return as being with the foreign domestics, not with the U.S. automakers.

- Suppliers overwhelmingly prefer working with Honda and Toyota.[1]

Here's a real-life example of how the adversarial game is played. Ford announced in 2003 a major reduction program to remove more than $3.2 billion in corporate costs. Because the company purchases more than half the value of its products from suppliers, it was natural and expected that the outside part and component makers would be approached to generate their share of the task. Ford formed 203 joint teams of engineers, buyers, and product people under a program called Total Value Management (TVM). The idea was to have these teams work with suppliers to find ways to reduce costs without hurting profit margins. This was the same philosophy that Chrysler used successfully in its SCORE program. But the reaction was more like GM got from Lopez than the favorable one Chrysler got with its approach.

The suppliers complained that the program's intent was distorted and warped because the teams were much more dictatorial and demanding in their one-on-one implementation. They accused Ford of setting benchmarks using unrealistic quotes from unqualified third sources. These prices were used to demand up-front reductions before the new parts were put into production.

Additionally, the entire savings were to be passed on to Ford, with no sharing to help the supplier margins. The result, reported by industry newspaper *Automotive News*, was that suppliers withheld ideas from Ford, and the program was bogged down in arguments and bad feelings.

The situation is clearly not confined to the beleaguered automobile makers. *Business Week* reported that the last remaining U.S. commercial airplane manufacturer, Boeing, is adopting a new approach with its suppliers as it looks to find ways to reduce the development and production costs of its new 7E7 Dreamliner jet.[2] Boeing and Airbus, in Europe, now control the world's commercial aerospace industry. This battle of U.S. versus European interests has an enormous impact on the health of the American industrial base because airplanes were our largest non-defense-related export in the recent decade. Boeing reportedly is asking suppliers to consider taking equity positions in the program and committing to significant and undefined cost reductions to get the plane approved and into development. The aerospace industry has always relied on specialized vendors and codevelopment as its model for growth. Now it appears that global political and cost pressures are pushing Boeing to become more aggressive and innovative in how it deals with its remaining domestic suppliers. The mutual future of both Boeing and its suppliers clearly rides on how both sides manage this change to avoid creating an adversarial situation.

Adversarial commerce is not limited just to manufacturing. The world's largest retailer, Wal-Mart, is taking increasingly tough stances with its supply chain as it dominates the mass-merchandising retail business. Its use of "everyday low prices" has successfully beaten Kmart, Sears, and other older merchandisers at the commercial game they invented. Wal-Mart is one of the masters in using point-of-sale data to communicate directly to its vendors, providing real-time information on how sales are moving back to their major suppliers. This reduces inventory and streamlines the flow of material and goods throughout the supply network. Wal-Mart supply chain–management techniques are being copied not only in retailing, but in manufacturing areas as well. But the business press has reported that the company's pressure on suppliers to pass on all the cost savings directly to Wal-Mart via price reductions is becoming more heavy handed and less friendly than the old way Sam Walton operated when he founded the company. Just as in the automotive and aerospace examples, the suppliers are having to adjust to a new management style that is more win/lose, take-it-or-leave-it, and more uncertain than in the past. Again, all of this is masked by the lofty goal of either recovering from economic hardship or, in Wal-Mart's case, continuing a very aggressive growth strategy. Suppliers are being pushed to "outsource" to overseas locations to provide the immediate cost relief to Wal-Mart. This topic became a subject of national debate during the 2004 presidential campaign.

It seems that adversarial behavior is exactly what the previous management members of American Airlines practiced when they withheld from their unions the fact that they had previously established a guaranteed severance benefit package for themselves when they were negotiating a concession package with their unions. American was threatening to file Chapter 11 bankruptcy to continue operations and used this threat to wring major wage and benefit concessions from its pilot, machinist, and attendant unions. Meanwhile, the senior officers had protected their own benefits in case the company had to go into bankruptcy. The public reaction to what appeared to be a purely adversarial act was so overwhelming it forced the CEO's resignation. Clearly, something in the American Airlines management culture encouraged this level of arrogance at the very time they needed cooperation. At the very least, it was considered ill timed and insensitive. But management approved it nonetheless, as a result of adversarial thinking.

Often this type of incident is dismissed as the result of odd (eccentric, if the person is rich) behavior by the individual in charge. The fact that it happens repeatedly in several different industries that cut across American business seems to indicate that the problem is more prevalent in management attitudes than in individual behavior.

The result of using increased adversarial management tactics at large corporations has increased the disruption in our domestic industrial economy and helped create an atmosphere of uncertainty regarding our nation's ability to compete. Instead of helping our industries become more competitive, these negative tactics could drive our industrial base off shore, further hurting our long-term economic revival and growth.

Command and Control Management Styles

These changes in management practices didn't just fall out of the sky in the last few years. How did we get into this situation, and why is it so prevalent in American business? The answer lies in our commercial history and tradition. It has been built into our method of commerce over hundreds of years. In many ways, it has become the standard model for business and the accepted norm. The command and control model of management has been followed for centuries in many different organizations, from religion to business; it certainly isn't new. This has become the standard model because it enjoyed success in the past—but that does not mean it will continue to work well in the future.

The term *command and control* is derived from military use, with decision making based on formal procedures that specifically define the limits of individual authority. In general management practice, it describes an organization that bases its decisions on a rigid and established hierarchy that is reflected in the firm's structure. The internal bureaucracy, in these cases, limits the amount of independence and autonomy that managers are given to operate. On the positive side, responses to problems are quick and follow predetermined answers. The disadvantages are that this limits flexibility and innovation. Throughout this book, the term *command and control* is used to describe centralized decision-making processes that are found in many established companies. These processes can often become unintentionally arbitrary and dictatorial. The term also is used to describe situations in which there is a standardized way of handling issues to force consistency across the organization. As a result, decisions are made at the top of the organization instead of at the lower levels.

The practice of treating the constituents of a firm (whether they are suppliers, dealers, employees, or managers) as enemies instead of allies cuts across all sectors. In many ways, this is done for expediency. The system sometimes isn't able to distinguish between firms that are the competition and ones that are necessary parts of the supply chain. This act of treating all in a unitary manner keeps management from having to spend time developing different strategies. We like consistency, so we treat everyone the same. The result is that sometimes we view employees in the same manner as competitors and inhibit building real alliances with them. We view shareholders with a degree of benign tolerance rather than as owners. Egos get in the way because we see everything as separate rather than part of a larger whole.

The use of command and control management has become so accepted and so widely practiced that, as managers, we seldom consider using other alternatives. Case studies and the business press have not only highlighted, but also encouraged, aggressive and sometimes ruthless management techniques. Business periodicals and academic institutions alike praised the chairmen of Enron and Tyco for their rapid and apparently innovative styles—at least, until their larger failings were uncovered and brought to light. Now the pendulum of reform is swinging the other way for corporate governance, but the momentum of the economy is still stuck in the historically negative ways of the past. It will take more than a few regulations and legislative changes to modify years of behavior that has encouraged companies to be separate and isolated. To illustrate, you need only look at how our business system operates and has developed over time.

A Condensed History of Commerce

The current system of commerce might not be perfect and could stand improvement going forward, but it certainly has the advantage of time on its side. Our ways of doing business between firms dates back to the beginning of trade itself. The manner in which the various entities are treated as distinct and separate elements has evolved over hundreds of years, during which people and institutions conducted business generally along a line that has remained unchanged. To better understand just how institutionalized the current approach is both in culture and in the minds of executives, we need to consider the way relationships between companies develop. We also need to look at why the separate elements of business and the people involved in managing them have resisted separation and why business relationships often remain very encumbered even today.

Throughout the Middle Ages, most production, with the exception of agriculture, was confined to craftsmen who single-handedly turned raw materials into finished goods. Armorers produced swords and protective suits out of steel that they processed themselves. Cobblers made shoes out of the basic material of hides, without any other intermediaries being involved. Supply chains were extremely simple and primarily provided basic raw materials to those craftsmen, who converted them into whatever manufactured products there were at the time. Most of this work was done in small single-person operations. Until the dawn of the Industrial Revolution, this simple conversion process limited most commercial operations to trading or bartering. But Western manufacturing remained constrained and largely self-contained. The process resisted changes in form even though it introduced new products. A similar analogy occurs today when companies use their old structure to try to enter new markets. The race to enter China is currently confusing many firms because their current organization might not work in the Chinese economy.

The Case of the Beaver Hat

The ways used to manage those early and simple supply chains began to form the basic DNA of what eventually became our modern commercial system. Take a look, for instance, at an example of early manufacturing to see how the seeds of independence were being sown. Consider the manufacture of the fur hats that were so popular in Europe in the 1700s. These hats were stylish products, and beaver fur was quite exotic and highly sought-after during this time.

The basic raw materials used were animal pelts provided by fur trappers roaming the remote areas of what later became Canada and the northern and western United States. These frontiersmen functioned as independent contractors working for themselves as they gathered or trapped the animals for their hides. They were the lowest level on the supply chain (unless you consider the beaver). These trappers sold their pelts to local outposts of trading companies, such as the Hudson Bay Company, which, in turn, transported them in bulk to markets in Europe. Upon arriving in Europe, the hides were sold to furriers who specialized in the inventory and distribution of the pelts to individual craftsmen. Those craftsmen then turned the hides into garments or other products, including the hugely popular beaver hat; in this case, a haberdasher made the final product and sold it in his own shop to the end consumer. This small yet efficient supply chain had at least five (six, if you still want to count the beaver) levels:

Beaver Hat Supply Chain

Consumer—Wealthy European customer

Haberdasher—Hat manufacturer and merchant

Furrier—Distributor of product

Trading company—Company that collects and transports material

Trapper—Individual collector

Beaver—Natural provider of raw material

This system worked well and satisfied the increasing demand for the highly styled product of beaver hats sold to a population of wealthy Europeans. But even in this most simple story from 300 years ago, we find examples of the problems of poor communication and lack of relationship among the distinct commercial elements involved in this basic business transaction.

Problems arose from poor and incomplete information among the various elements. The trapper, not knowing that the demand for beaver was rising over the other animals, often did not understand the value of his catch. He trapped and sold whatever he could, with little or no knowledge of how it would be used or its relative value at final assembly. To him, the only distinction in pricing was the natural mix of beavers versus the other animals that he caught; he did not know about the demand for the pelt. If he had known, he might have elected to hold out for a higher price for the popular fur.

The trading company had more knowledge and, hence, more power in negotiation. It was able to view the source of supply from a larger perspective because it dealt with many trappers over a wider area. But it, too, was limited by the time it took to transport the material back to Europe and because it was involved in businesses other than just fur trading. The trading company's job was to get the material to Europe as quickly as possible. The distributor had more intimate knowledge of the demand and could adjust his prices based on inventory of the pelts. Finally, although the haberdasher saw the demand for his final product, he had to rely on the rest of the chain for information on the availability of his raw material. Basically, everyone was operating in the dark, and the only contact was with the next immediate level in the chain.

In this example, each element really operated independently and passed on little information to the next link in the chain. Clearly, the lowest end of the chain, the trapper, never saw the end-user market for his product and probably never saw or realized the larger markups that each step was compounding on his product as it worked its way through the production system. But, then, trappers might not have been as aggressive as today's executives and perhaps were satisfied just to earn a subsistence-level wage. The trapper would have to wait about 250 years for stock options or grants to come into the picture.

Commerce didn't really change much with the advancement of the Industrial Age. Even in its earliest fashion, commerce was based on individual elements or levels, with little communication or coordination between them. Clearly, a hundred years ago, communication was less easy and speedy than it is today, so the system actually worked fairly well. But the bad habits and the protected independence of the companies started to be built into the permanent fabric of commercial dealings.

Using this example, you can substitute things such as steel for pelts, warehouse distributors for the furriers, and final manufacturers for the haberdasher. They are really very similar in process—just much more complex and with many more levels and separate elements. The point is that not much has changed through the ages. In today's business world, managers and companies often operate "in the dark," just as the trapper did, not understanding or knowing what happens above or below in the corporate chain.

The basic process is the same today, whether the product is a car, a DVD player, a Twinkie, or a beaver hat. The separate tiers of the chain don't talk to more than the next level, at best, and the primary form of communication between companies is the exchange of goods for money. We trade invoices for checks and not much else. Each level assumes its own risk and shares nothing else along the way. It has worked for literally hundreds of years and is the basis for the capitalistic system that we all enjoy. Economists will tell you that it is the most efficient way to allocate resources, and some political parties have based their entire platform on protecting this concept.

The Problem of Isolation

As the commercial system evolved, companies were formed and became larger, more complicated entities. The emergence of the public corporation, whose shares in the company are held by anonymous owners widely scattered across the country, helped encourage the isolation of management from other businesses that they needed to survive. Emerging businesses often rely on a close network of related or supporting companies to offer specialized work or help extend the operation of a startup or a new firm. That's why firms within a given industry generally locate close together, as with automakers in the Midwest around Detroit, steel manufacturers in Pittsburgh, high-technology software firms in Silicon Valley, and aerospace in Seattle and also Kansas. As American business grew in the twentieth century, its largest industries tended to centralize in geographic pockets within the country. This was beneficial because it permitted the growth of supporting companies to also co-locate in those areas and service the entire industry. Entire supporting "farm teams" of vendors and specialized suppliers were built around these basic industries and grew in places such as Akron, Detroit, Pittsburgh, Wichita, and other centers of industry.

This geographic centralization of business obviously helped in making logistics and communication easier and closer as the industries grew. But there was also a downside to this geographic concentration: It helped create an isolated and parochial management outlook in those industries. In effect, the management of the leading manufacturers isolated the companies in centralized enclaves. The major players surrounded themselves with companies that relied on them for their own existence. In many ways, this geographic isolation permitted the adaptation of unique styles of management with a given industry. By having such a close physical location, it permitted the management of the dominant players in each industry to build a pseudo–caste society similar to what existed in Europe during the Middle Ages. This isolation might have some good points, but it also established a corporate culture of isolating the firm from those that it is actually dependent upon and turns it into an elitist model. Bob Lutz, my predecessor as president of Chrysler and now vice chairman of General Motors, uses an analogy of medieval times to describe the situation in business.

As a company grows in size and importance in its industry, it might act like the king in a feudal caste system. The company behaves much like the king, living in a castle protected by policies and power, isolated physically from the workers surrounding his enterprise. The lowly workers, or serfs, spend their time toiling for the benefit of the king and are able to keep only a small portion of their production. Each month, they labor in the fields or at their crafts and bring their harvest and goods up the hill to the castle, where they are taxed heavily and dismissed to begin the process all over again. Each month, they toil away for the benefit of the feudal master, who treats the serfs as lesser beings but tolerates them as economic necessities under his complete control. This feudal analogy is not too far removed from the way many major American industrial firms operate. They view themselves as masters of their operation that extends to the suppliers, dealers, and employees. They do not reach out to the firms that are necessarily supporting them. This is a control-oriented system that is effective but not optimized. The concentration is on the manner of control instead of cooperation, and the emphasis is on direction instead of independent thought.

It is into this closed, isolated society of business that the dangers of adversarial behavior can develop and spread. Because the structure is so interwoven and the players so mutually dependent, the caste system of dominant and submissive companies encourages the emergence of negative and harsh tactics. The leaders of a given industry know that the contracts they hand out create an extremely strong economic reliance by the supporting companies. Yet these supporting companies are also isolated from each other by their extremely competitive nature and desire to manage their own destiny.

The supporting companies are often so closely related to one of the major manufacturers that they have not sought business from other companies. As long as the industry and the major company grew, the supporting firms were sucked along in the wake and often enjoyed the ride. Some of the mansions that to this day surround the suburbs of major industrial cities were often built by the owners of these closely related subordinate supply companies. While the growth continued, everyone benefited. The supported firms did not band together as the labor unions did, to obtain the counter-veiling power that John K. Galbraith cited as the economic reason for union growth in these larger industries. The supplier firms were content to exist on the lucrative handouts and contracts that the major firms issued. Trade associations provided only limited voice or position for these many smaller companies. The only response was limited consolidation in some areas of the business, but most industries today have remained relatively fragmented.

In this closed feudal system that still exists today in almost all large industries, managing the relationships can turn ugly. The

analogy to the feudal system is very useful. In some cases, a benev-
olent king or ruler watched out for the welfare of the supporting
serfs and workers. But in other cases, darker personalities concentrated on the harder side of control and suppression of ideas. As
our industrial fortunes ride the economic roller coaster of the markets, the pressure to revert to more demands, more direction, and
less coordination is very tempting to managers who are trying to
fix their bottom line. The isolation and separation that has historically been built into our commercial system is helping to accelerate
the use of adversarial commerce. The strong built-in tendency for
management to use the old style of command and control, even in
new high-technology industries, continues as an accepted and validated way to manage, both internally and externally. If left
unchanged, adversarial techniques used to manage important
relationships between companies will continue to sap the strength
of our industrial base and erode our ability to compete against
lower-cost areas of the world.

Endnotes

1. PPI press release dated May 2, 2004.

2. Holmes, Stanley. "A Plane, A Plan, A Problem," *Business Week*
   1 December 2003: http://zdnet.businessweek.com.

3

ENDING ADVERSARIAL COMMERCE

Inefficiencies in the Current System

Everywhere we look, it appears that our established American industrial firms are under attack from more nimble and responsive competition. It comes equally from new small domestic startup firms as from foreign companies entering our domestic markets. These firms can challenge the existing model in several areas of apparent weakness: They are less prone to follow our time-honored business traditions. They can be faster and, because they are relatively new, can operate with less structure and bureaucracy. Our well-established system has too many separate layers and transactions. The flow of goods, material, and information is hampered by the fact that the atmosphere between the parties is more adversarial than it needs to be.

While I was running procurement and supply for Chrysler, we spent some time looking at just how screwed up the system was. After diving into the picture, it turned out to be a lot more complicated than any of us realized.

The Roller Lifter Story

We had our supply group at Chrysler select one of the simplest parts that went into a car and then used it as an example of how complicated supply chains really are. The group selected a mundane little part called a roller lifter, a 2-inch-long machined metal component used in the valve train of an engine. If the roller lifter fails, the intake or exhaust valve fails to open or close and the engine misses or loses power. In addition, its failure pushes the emissions system out of legal compliance. In other words, this is critical and a vital part. The device was purchased from Eaton Corp., which sold it to Chrysler for about $2 each.

Working with the supply people at Eaton Corp., our people used an increasingly popular technique to "map" the chains of companies and events that went into the total production process of this part. We detailed each step, starting with Chrysler receiving the part and moving backward as far as possible through the processes in the entire production cycle for the roller lifter. The resulting study amazed all of us, even those who knew the product was more complicated than it appeared. Figure 3.1 shows the complete mapped chain of the roller lifter. This figure shows that this one simple part is actually made up of 12 separate subcomponents, including springs, seals, washers, and roller bearings. As the end user, at Chrysler, we had paid no real attention to where these sub-components came from because we assumed that Eaton either made most of them or closely controlled them. Actually, Eaton mainly did the final machining and assembly of the part and relied on many subsuppliers for critical operations outside Eaton's plants.

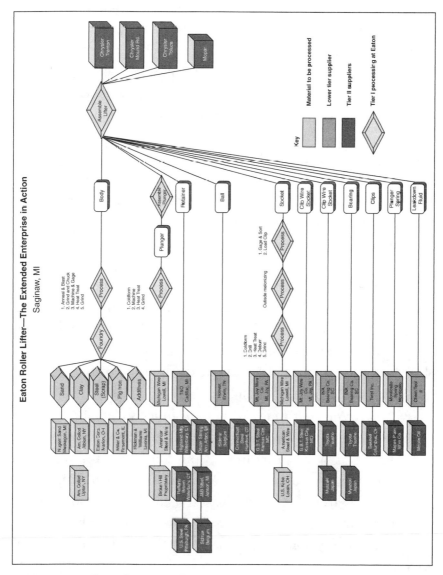

Figure 3.1—Roller Lifter Example

When we investigated the origin of all 12 subcomponents, it turned out that this single part from one supplier actually was a complicated web of parts that came from more than 33 individual companies. That massive figure was rolled into a thing that cost less than $2. The supply chain includes the raw material used in making steel, the drawing of wire to make springs, and the ball bearings. Just for fun, we then traced every single item, including the raw materials used in making this relatively simple part.

We started with raw materials that naturally come from the Earth. Our first raw material subsupplier for the roller lifter, the American Colloid Company, is one of the world's leading suppliers of bentonite clay. That's a commodity that appears in thousands of products, including auto parts, building material, diapers, and even kitty litter. In fact, we found out that the company sells as much clay to cat owners as it does to car companies. Imagine the feeling in Detroit that we were in some small way competing with kitty litter manufacturers for a commodity.

After the American Colloid people scoop up the bentonite that will eventually form part of the roller lifter, they ship it to their plant in central Michigan for processing. When they're finished, the refined clay is sent to a foundry about a hundred miles away. The foundry uses lots of other raw materials in a process to anneal, blast, grind, machine, and heat-treat the housing of the roller lift and ship it to Eaton to be assembled and sent to Chrysler.

But the chain isn't finished. Lots of other subcomponents are involved. Plungers come from two sources, one in Ohio and one in Australia. Add a retainer from Connecticut, a bearing from Tennessee, and cast sockets from Missouri, along with clips from Japan, springs from Ohio, and leak test fluid from Illinois. It all ends up in an Eaton plant near Detroit for final assembly.

By this point, you might be amazed by the complicated chain of events. So were we. The whole process involved no fewer than 33 companies. The seemingly simple act of building one small part for one engine turned out to be incredibly complex. Now multiply this for every part in a car (there are more than 5,000 parts in a finished car), and you can see why the auto industry touches so many companies and employees around the country. It is truly a massive extended enterprise that employs more people than any other manufacturing industry.

That fact so amazed our staff that we started to call all the suppliers involved along the chain to see if they knew what was happening to their product. We called one of our distant suppliers who made one component of the roller lifter. When he found out we were calling from Chrysler, he said, "Gosh, my wife loves her Grand Cherokee!" So we questioned whether he knew if his part had a critical role in his wife's safety. We told him the thing he made went to a guy who did something else with it and then sent it to someone else, who did another thing with it and then sent it to one of our engine plants—and if that part didn't work, his wife's engine would die.

He said, "Nope. I never know where that stuff goes after I ship it." That comment is indicative of what happens all the time. Smaller companies almost never know that their product is ultimately going to Chrysler or any other large manufacturer. That's because the different tiers in the supply chain traditionally don't communicate with each other through any medium other than purchase orders.

The management of these companies really rarely ever has a clue about where they fit into the bigger picture. They run their companies from a perspective that they are isolated—and if they do know their place in the chain, they often assume that they have no real impact on it. More often than not, the commercial system forces companies to remain distant and separate from each other. The companies make a product and ship it to someone else. The communication is limited and seldom involves anything more than shipping or pricing information. When management does get involved, it often turns negative because it usually means that problems exist. This is a consistent trait of adversarial management or culture: The managers rarely get involved unless there is a problem.

This illustrates the problems that exist in the way we currently manage the enterprise of business. It shows how seemingly unrelated companies travel through time without really knowing how they affect other companies. This remoteness is complicated by the fact that the companies are all independent from each other in purpose, mission, management, planning, and communication.

Because we value our independence so dearly in this country, our businesses operate with a fierce sense of separation and single-mindedness. That is one reason acquisitions are favored over alliances. We seem to have a natural inclination to run our own show and look like we are in control of our own destiny. As the roller lifter story shows, the truth is that companies are much more interrelated than their management might want to believe or might even know.

Problems Created by Adversarial Commerce

Adversarial commerce has become so entrenched as the way business operates that we often are not aware of its cost or the problems it can create. Certainly, its use is not very often intentional or deliberate; it seems to build up over time within companies without an overt decision to adopt some of the associated behavior. Understanding that it is often subtle, or hidden, might help businesses understand some of the more serious situations that can occur. At least four major business attributes drive the trend toward adversarial commerce: distrust, poor communication, limited planning, and a constant quest for complete control. These ultimately add costs to the way of doing business and slow the response to changes that occur in the marketplace. Not only are their deleterious effects costing companies money—they also are the main items hampering change.

Problem 1: Distrust and Suspicion

"All I want is a little trust, but you know it don't come easy." I'm sure that Ringo Starr wasn't referring to business when he put that line in one of his few solo hits, "It Don't Come Easy," but it is true just same. The first major problem is that the historical independence between companies sometimes forces them to view each other with suspicion instead of trust. Business is controlled more by quotes and a bidding process than by long-standing relationships. This is the result of concern over building conflicts in a relationship between two firms. To avoid the appearance of any conflict of interest between supplying firms, most companies have policies that ensure at least three competitive bids in any major new transaction. This practice can turn every project or purchase into a standalone event without continuity or long-range planning. As a result, distrust arises between companies that should be working more closely together.

Trust is essential to any relationship, but our present system actually inhibits rather than builds it. Think back to the GM/Lopez story. The supplier community accused Lopez of taking proprietary drawings from one source and sending them to another for quotation (among other transgressions). The new source did not have to recoup its development and engineering expenditure, as the original did. When word of this action came out, the automotive community rose up in arms against GM and threatened legal action. An enormous amount of mistrust was created between GM and its suppliers. This was one of the first things that Lopez's replacement, Rick Wagoner, set out to rebuild.

If mistrust and suspicion replace a trusting environment in business, both parties respond by building in protective mechanisms to ensure that their respective interests are protected at all costs. Adversarial actions—such as canceling contracts without proper notice, using unqualified sources for low quotes, inflating costs on a project to avoid paying royalties or other payments, or pursuing legal actions to intimidate or threaten—contribute to mistrust between companies. Although most companies do not resort to completely suspending further business when they mistrust another, they often make sure that pricing to the other company reflects the element of risk and difficulty experienced in the past. That is why, under the Extended Enterprise®, we worked hard at Chrysler to create an atmosphere in which our actions were predictable and consistent. Those are the elements that build trust and permit companies to create long-lasting relationships.

It takes a lot of time to rebuild an environment of trust after it has been damaged. But many large companies seem to care less about creating trust than about using adversarial tactics to gain what appear to be advantages, even though these often prove to be short-term advantages. Many company financial systems often give more weight to maintaining current cost situations than to saving money in the future. The time-honored present value technique always favors a dollar saved today over one saved tomorrow. One reason for this is that future costs cannot be exactly quantified as much as current ones can. Thus, companies pay less attention to items such as warranty than to the piece price (the term used in the auto industry to mean the price for an individual part or piece) because warranty is a consideration of the future.

As many companies are finding now, much like adversarial actions, these future costs come home to roost eventually. Costs such as warranty and lost customer loyalty are very hard and expensive to reverse when they finally are recognized.

Problem 2: Poor Communication

The second problem is that, despite major innovations in data processing, meaningful communication remains poor and spotty throughout many supply chains. Using computers to pass order and shipping information between links in the chain has ushered in enormous advancements in productivity. Just-in-time shipments have reduced inventory requirements and improved quality in many manufacturing businesses. Shipments are now made hourly into some assembly plants, with the parts sequenced at the same pace as the production line. This has all been beneficial, and the advantages have helped boost productivity in the United States. But this communication is between one computer and another computer, and does not usually involve human judgment or analysis. Hierarchy and policy still control and limit communication between executives and between middle management in companies. This same control logic makes some companies leery of becoming too close to other companies and establishing useful relationships.

Negative actions and the desire for independence come out clearly in the way companies communicate with each other. The roller lifter example shows that sometimes the only communication between firms is through an invoice and the resulting check for payment. That might be fine for commodity-type purchases or something that is not critical to the operation—no one really expects a company to share its inner plans and goals with its supplier of pencils or sandwiches in the cafeteria. Beyond such routine cases, however, the need for accurate and complete information is vital to any business relationship.

Some time-tested adversarial items here include spoon-feeding only information that is absolutely necessary to land a contract; ordering more than planned to get a discount, only to revise the order later under some pretext of change; sending notification that a project has been canceled just before doing so; and dabbling in all sorts of other mischief. Again, much of this information control is done to keep the other party at odds or in tension. If the company's actions get to be too predictable or too visible, the subordinate party might decide to take independent actions that the dominant one might not want. An example of this is discounting anticipated volumes if the sales drop. Companies such as Wal-Mart provide real-time access to sales directly to their vendors so that they can see how material is moving and can help manage inventory. Wal-Mart might use some high-pressure leverage on pricing, but the company clearly sees the advantage of transparency in business information. I found an example of the opposite when I ran MSX International.

For six years from the initial launch in 1996 until its final production run in 2002, MSX had painted every Plymouth Prowler for Chrysler. This was a low-volume specialty vehicle that we had taken from concept to production in less than three years while I was at Chrysler. The car was never intended for high volume, so the painting operation was outsourced to MSX to reduce the internal investment. MSX operated a dedicated, labor-intensive facility that painted the primed aluminum bodies and shipped them to Chrysler so they could be made into vehicles, much like the way the industry operated in the early 1920s.

Because the project never was intended to be long term, MSX took a five-year lease on the paint plant. As the Prowler entered its fifth year, the fickleness of the specialty car market caused sales to drop, creating a glut of inventory. Having been one of the concept originators, I called my old employer to ask if folks there were planning to cancel production. I was told that they were planning to keep it for at least another year. Based on this commitment, we renewed our lease on the plant and extended our labor contract with our union. Sales continued to drop, and the car was suddenly cancelled only three months later. Chrysler ended up paying much more in cancellation to us than it would have if we had all discussed the situation openly. But Chrysler was so afraid that word would get out that the car would be terminated, that the news was kept from everyone, including dealers, who were stuck with more than a year's worth of finished cars in their inventory. Usually, sharing information can reduce costs, whereas protecting it can create unnecessary ones.

Problem 3: Lack of Joint Planning

The third problem area arises when there is little or limited shared planning and advance development. Too few companies now share their future plans with the members of their supply chain that they have built to support them. Many industrial companies do their advance planning in secret, fearing that plans will leak to their competition. After the plans are developed and approved, the project is sent to the engineering department to be designed. Only after that task is completed are outside partners brought into the process. The whole process is too sequential and, in many cases, similar to the beaver hat chain explored in the last chapter, in which the chain was not united into a common goal or purpose.

The quest for independence and control also can contribute to a reluctance of companies to plan jointly. Instead of sharing a marketing plan or pricing strategy for a new product to facilitate ideas and galvanize others around a project, many companies keep their dealers, vendors, and often even key employees in the dark about the objectives of a new project. True, many aspects might require confidentiality, but this is often used as a convenient excuse to avoid most joint planning. The other companies then are not prepared to react as quickly or to contribute resources to the project. They operate in the dark and often don't know whether their customers will accept the new products they work on after they fund and complete the project.

In an ideal situation, companies would work closely together to define future product needs. Wish lists defining joint development objectives would give suppliers the necessary security to commit to their own research projects. For example, a computer company could outline what it needs in new hard drive technology and work with its suppliers to have them develop the device. A consumer electronics company might outline the type of microprocessor it needs to offer a smaller DVD recorder. A car company could define a tire that would still run if it lost pressure, thus eliminating the spare tire. In each case, the new product is either a feature or a component incorporated into a larger item manufactured by the dominant or major company. These purchasing companies would commit to incorporating the device if the supplying firm successfully developed it. This joint planning and sourcing would reduce the larger company's outlay for research and development and would ensure a less risky, more secure return for the supplier.

It might sound simple, but in practice, this type of sharing is discouraged under adversarial commerce. If the company auctions the new product to a lower bidder or deletes its requirement without compensating the company, the resulting mistrust can stop further developments. The old expression "Once burned, twice shy" holds true in business just as in personal lives. The result, in this case, would be increased development costs and reduced speed to market for the dominant company. When the atmosphere between the companies becomes poisoned by negative actions and uncertainty, the cost of doing business between them increases. All this is unnecessary if management were more open and cooperated in more joint planning. We just have to change the mindset that corporations must have so many secrets that they need to protect from allied partners. Obviously, it is wise to keep company plans from competitors, but that doesn't mean partners should be equally kept in the dark. Firms that deal with several major clients, such as advertising, engineering, consulting, and research, all have shown that they can protect the corporate secrets of their clients, especially because breaking that bond would mean losing future business or damaging their reputation in the market place. The main reason companies continue to keep too much information too close to their vests is to exercise tight control over their partners.

Problem 4: Tendency Toward Complete Control

The fourth trouble spot involves constant pressure for "control" of the process. The prevailing organizational mindset of most industrial companies is to be in complete control of a project or operation. Complete ownership is preferred over joint ventures, and acquisitions are preferred over alliances because that keeps control close at hand. The real reasons are often masked under the cloak of financial measures, but the truth is that it is easier to own something than to work jointly in a project or to share power with others. It is easier to manage, to make decisions, and to decide strategy when you have control over a company than when you have to share that power with another partner in a venture.

The greatest problem that adversarial commerce brings is escalation in the amount of control exercised throughout the company, both internally and externally. Control is a natural state that all people strive to achieve, and it is the same for corporations. We all like to be in a stable environment in which we primarily decide our own actions. Managers in corporations want the same, and they often use control tactics to try to stabilize and direct the business. Most people are disturbed by uncertainty; to remove that condition, managers often gravitate to using more aggressive command and control styles. Strong control systems have been built into our organizations, from very early examples including the military and the Catholic Church. It is no accident that our commercial system uses similar rules and direction to establish some degree of control.

To a large extent, we have been conditioned and educated to accept some amount of control from the proper authority. In business, this authority usually comes from the fact that someone is buying a good or service. For example, if someone pays an architect to design a home, the client has a right to expect that he has some control over that design and that the architect knows he is not completely free to do whatever he wants. Because the client paid for the service, he has a right to expect that he can control it, and the provider expects that he must satisfy the customer. This traditional condition has become protected in commercial codes and law over time.

Problems arise when the manner and tone of control gets too one-sided, too arbitrary, and often too illogical for the other party to accept. In these cases, using control steps beyond trying to bring order to the relationship and moves into trying to dominate it. In my current company, I have found a long history of this type of action in our negotiations.

Before I joined MSX, the company had established a joint venture with a minority partner to pursue business under an industry-wide initiative to expand minority businesses. The problem was MSX wanted to control the venture even though, by regulation, we had to own less than 50 percent. So we brought in a third party to hold 2 percent, making the final makeup 49 percent minority, 49 percent MSX, and 2 percent third neutral party (who happened to be a minority businessman with extremely close ties to MSX). This clearly defeated both the intent of the venture and threatened the actual certification of it as a minority company because majority ownership was not resting in any one party. Fortunately for MSX, the venture never really got off the ground—and one of the main reasons was our overwhelming concern for control. When I questioned our managers who set up the idea, they were floored that I would challenge the concept because they thought they were being imaginative in protecting our "interests."

Conflicts over control are common today because large companies sometimes mouth the words of mutual co-existence and partnership but still seek ways, as MSX did, to ensure that they have the final say in what happens. The current trend in industry is to tell employees and suppliers that they have more authority to manage their own decisions. But these statements cannot ring true if the buying company maintains its old-style monitoring and financial control reporting structure—the old financially dominated system that required a staff group outside of the operating management to review everything. This defeats the purpose of letting people or suppliers manage their own actions. This act of not "letting go" of the military-like review is one of the most damaging effects of adversarial commerce.

These four problem aspects—distrust, poor communication, lack of planning, and desire for absolute control—are present in most industrial organizations today. They help distort management's thinking and influence behaviors in a negative manner. They create waste by increasing the hidden costs of running a business. These are the types of decisions that are made daily in big companies primarily because these companies have a culture and ethic of wanting complete control. This comes with a high price that cannot be absorbed in industries such as automobiles that are under competitive threat from other manufacturers overseas that do not follow such philosophies.

Impact on Management Style

The impact of each of these four issues is magnified in their effect on our management system. Their cumulative effect is to isolate the firm from within and to turn the management culture into a more negative and adversarial one than is either necessary or productive. Using the example of the old U.S. Big Three manufacturing philosophy that the companies needed to make almost everything that is used in a car, you can see how that attitude evolved into one that did not trust outside suppliers. The logic was flawed, and it is not limited to the automotive companies. Many industries have gone through a similar mutation of culture that has caused them to mistrust not only their supply chain, but also their own rank-and-file employees. Management's approach to its suppliers and its own unions has often turned into one that approaches the feudal king analogy.

   This attitude is present in many companies. Suppliers are "tolerated" as long as they act subservient to the larger company and treat them with the proper deference. One reason companies are suspicious of the increasing power that large global suppliers hold is that they fear the fact that the supplier also deals with their competitors. These large suppliers, such as Bosch and Denso, count literally all of the world's automakers on each of their customer lists. On one hand, the automakers say they want suppliers that are global and serve the whole industry instead of ones that supply to only one firm. But they also have admitted that they fear that a supplier with a larger share at the competition will be more influenced by that larger commercial relationship. This is an unnatural fear because, although these companies claim to want independence, they also demand allegiance. Suppliers are confused; as a result, the current adversarial style drives what should be a close working relationship further apart.

The same situation occurs in dealings with the unions at a company. Senior management often complains about the union position being opposite to its own, when both should actually be working to implement the same thing: profits generated through production of goods. Yet the history of labor relations is characterized by adversarial behavior in many industries, from automobiles to airlines, telecommunications to trucking.

The issues are similar in the treatment of both unions and suppliers. Large corporations establish internal departments to handle the unique relationship issues found in their labor relations and procurement areas. Although these specialized departments do manage the functions effectively, they also intentionally isolate the CEO and other senior management officials from both groups. The primary channel of communication to the top of the company is through these well-established and powerful departments. In most industrial companies, it is an unwritten rule that the CEO is not supposed to deal directly with the head of the union or the head of a supplier on business issues without involving the vice president of the respective departments. This practice can isolate the CEO and remove him from the real complexity of running his business. It also contributes to the CEO's possible belief that his company is more distinct than it really is in an extended enterprise situation.

Adversarial Commerce Limits Growth

The problems that adversarial commerce creates and its impact on the style of management can actually limit the growth and competitiveness of the firm. With complicated and interrelated supply chains, no mature company can continue to operate in the isolation that it might have had in its early stages. But the communication problems and quest for complete control often slow the ability of a company caught up in negative tactics to respond to new competitors. Before you think that this logic is unique to a particular company, we need to look at how widespread its application really is; we do that in the next chapter.

4

WHERE IN THE WORLD IS ADVERSARIAL COMMERCE?

You don't have to look hard to find evidence of adversarial commerce: You can find it in most industries and many companies. It might not be intentional and might be a result of policies that were actually intended to "protect" a firm's financial situation. Although this business approach is not everywhere, certain factors help foster the right conditions to make it flourish. Identifying these elements and characteristics can help isolate where it might occur and avoid its problems.

Bad Customer Relations

Adversarial tactics are not necessarily confined to dealings with suppliers. They also can occur with other related parties, such as dealers and employees. They can even impact customers, who are the very heart of a company's existence. Healthcare providers are a good example of this. The relationship among the insurance providers, the physicians who deliver the care, and the patient who receives treatment is under constant tension. This tension often turns ugly when selected entities use more aggressive tactics than normal.

Patients often must follow extremely complex and rigid rules to receive treatment. They find themselves in endless circles of paperwork to provide proof of eligibility or valid enrollment. The process has been automated in many places to be more efficient, but it still often results in delays in payment to providers or rejected patient claims after treatment. Instead of being user-friendly, the approval and reimbursement system is notorious for supporting a bureaucracy that measures success on the delay of cash reimbursement.

According to the *Wall Street Journal*[1], hospitals rank among America's most aggressive debt collectors because they put increasing pressure on poor and uninsured patients to pay their bills. Hospitals are resorting to the most adversarial means of debt collection: actually arresting patients who don't pay. Although other financial institutions have moved away from using such harsh tactics, the *Journal* reports that some of our nation's hospitals have resorted to increased use of extreme legal procedures to settle open debts.

These same hospitals have further alienated their patients and the government by charging uninsured patients more than those who have insurance coverage such as Medicare or private policies. The American Hospital Association claimed in December 2003 that existing regulations of Medicare forced the hospitals into aggressive pricing at full cost for their uninsured patients. Finally, the Secretary of Health and Human Services had to issue an official administrative response to the hospitals to get them to stop the practice and to "assist the uninsured and underinsured." Clearly, the hospital actions in these cases can be classified as adversarial toward the very patients they are supposed to serve.

As reported in the *Wall Street Journal*, the common hospital practice of charging uninsured patients more than those who have insurance coverage and then arresting those who fail to pay (known as "body attachment") has brought pressure for reform from several states. Hospital industry organizations have strongly resisted such efforts. For example, in California, a bill in 2003 that would have protected patients from "aggressive billing and collections was shelved following heavy industry opposition."[1] Clearly, not all hospitals are following such adversarial practices, but it is frequent enough to have raised pressure of reform from the press and litigation. It shows that this type of negative behavior can impact customers directly.

Another more blatant example occurred in the airline industry in 1999. This was before the 9/11 disaster, which severely impacted the financial health of the major carriers. The airline industry has been in some degree of financial difficulty for the past few decades. It is predictable that, in that climate, adversarial behavior can occur.

On January 3, 1999, the Midwestern states experienced a snowfall with historic results. During that day, more than 24 inches of snow fell on places such as Chicago, Detroit, and Cleveland. Northwest Airlines operated one of its three central hubs out of Detroit, where a majority of flights and passengers are located.

Northwest controls more than 75 percent of all air traffic in and out of Detroit; the airline has a clear dominant position and resists competition aggressively. When there is little choice left to consumers, sometimes companies adopt an attitude of indifference toward their own clients.

During this historic snowfall, although other carriers suspended or diverted flights, Northwest continued to order its planes to land in Detroit, in an effort to avoid stranding them in other less centrally located cities. Unfortunately, through a combination of unintended errors by both Northwest and the airport staff at Detroit's Wayne County Metropolitan Airport, thousands of passengers were trapped on planes that had landed and were unable to unload at the terminal. Some people were kept locked in their planes for more than 11 hours before the airport could plow the runways and clear the gates to permit the planes to unload. The condition on the planes was intolerable. The passengers were trapped inside, with exhausted food supplies and toilets overflowing into the aisles. People with medical conditions were unable to get to the prescriptions they had checked in their luggage. Cell phone calls to newspapers and TV stations brought the situation to the public. It was a disaster that made headlines around the nation, and it severely inconvenienced the captive clientele of Northwest.

Initially, Northwest resisted any attempt to repair the damage to their customers. The company claimed the storm was an act of God and that it was not responsible for the airport operation. Both facts were accurate. But the public reaction was one of rage directed at Northwest for poor planning. To make matters worse, Northwest was pressured by the media reports and legal action by irate travelers to compensate those people who were inconvenienced by the airline's adversarial approach to its customers. It was forced to settle a class action lawsuit by paying more than $7.1 million on behalf of more than 7,000 passengers who were affected by its actions. Fortunately for Northwest, the company seems to have learned from this experience and has shown significant improvement in customer satisfaction after this unfortunate incident. It has changed from its more callous ways and become much more customer oriented. The experience remains an example of how company policies might be more negative than actually intended. In this case, it appears that Northwest has learned a company's response to what was an act of nature has the real possibility of turning negative without any such intention.

Kmart's Adversarial Policies

The retailing business provides another example of how firms can resort to negative practices instead of trying to solve the basic problem. During its ill-fated attempt to meet the competitive threat from Wal-Mart's Everyday Low Price (ELP) policy, Kmart initiated a similar program in 2001 called Blue Light Always. I served on the Kmart board during this difficult time, and I gained firsthand exposure to the situation. Wal-Mart's ELP strategy is to consistently offer the lowest price against all national competition instead of relying on promotional discounts as Kmart did. Customers learned that by shopping at Wal-Mart regularly, they would get lower prices without having to shop for the deal of the day that Kmart pushed. Wal-Mart had developed ELP as a corporate strategy over many years, going back to the original philosophy of Sam Walton, the firm's founder. Kmart had invented the discount model in the 1950s and 1960s, but it had continued to use promotional pricing to get people into its stores, where normal goods were priced 3–4 percent above those at Wal-Mart. Customers began turning to Wal-Mart in mass exodus.

To monitor and control ELP, Wal-Mart uses an elaborate and sophisticated inventory-control system that tracks the point of sale of every item in every store on a real-time basis. For example, the company knows each night just how many tubes of Crest toothpaste were sold that day by flavor, type, and size. The Wal-Mart information technology systems feed that real data back to suppliers such as Procter & Gamble who can see what products are moving and adjust inventories accordingly. Using the information from this system, Wal-Mart and its suppliers are able to predict levels of sales more accurately than competitors such as Kmart, who still labor under 20-year-old, out-of-date IT systems.

Wal-Mart used its better sales information to negotiate better payment terms from its suppliers. By providing suppliers with accurate forecasts for purchases, Wal-Mart was able to prove that doing business with Wal-Mart was easier and more predictable. Suppliers agreed to longer payment cycles, too, because they had confidence that the sales-planning data would be accurate and that Wal-Mart would pay its bills promptly. Kmart wanted to get a similar advantage of extended terms to provide better cash flow. In response, it launched a program to directly match Wal-Mart head to head in pricing on both promotional and routine-purchase items. The problem was, Kmart did not have an IT system that could provide the accurate forecasting and inventory ordering that Wal-Mart used. Kmart launched into Blue Light Always in desperation to stem dropping sales, even though it did not have the necessary information to show its supplier the progress of sales. The result is historic.

Kmart's management outlined a program of limited manual price adjustment to launch the program. Because it represented a radical change in strategy, management decided to start slowly so they could monitor the early results. These lower prices were intended to stimulate demand and boost overall store sales and revenue. As the program expanded beyond what management could handle manually, they had to rely on the IT system to implement the necessary price changes. All of these changes created so much activity that the Kmart system was put into overload and crashed. Invoices piled up and material was sent to the wrong stores, only to sit in inventory. Sales under Blue Light Always continued to fall rather than increase. The experiment was such a failure that it is considered one of the reasons Kmart had to declare bankruptcy in January 2002.

The internal reaction within Kmart to the confusion created by the Blue Light Always experiment had major repercussions on its suppliers. Instead of producing sales data and positive results to use in negotiating extended terms, the confusion had the opposite effect. Suppliers started reducing shipments to keep from increasing their receivables to Kmart. Rumors of slow payment by Kmart started to appear in the local Detroit papers. Instead of working more closely with its suppliers, Kmart was moving toward a much more adversarial situation with them.

In late 2001, the Kmart board cautioned senior management that this could create an explosive situation. Every company needs the cooperation of its suppliers to survive. The experience at Chrysler had proven that even during a financial crisis, suppliers can respond and rally behind a company in trouble if there is open communication of the situation. Unfortunately, those in Kmart management either never got this point or chose to ignore it. Several months later, the cash situation became so tight that suppliers refused to continue to ship goods, forcing Kmart to declare bankruptcy in January 2002.

Many other unrelated issues beyond poor supplier communication and relations brought Kmart into bankruptcy. Many of these were later revealed in a detailed investigation that the board conducted, but because of continued litigation, those issues will have to wait for open discussion. The fact remains, however, that Kmart did not seize the opportunity to work more closely with its supply chain and resorted instead to using extremely adversarial methods. No one can say that if Kmart had operated under a more collaborative approach, it could have prevented bankruptcy, but following the adversarial approach certainly didn't help avoid it. The new surviving company appears to have learned from this experience: Kmart is reportedly working to improve relationships with its dedicated suppliers even though it continues to lose market share.

An Industry Comparison

By most measures, the U.S. automobile companies tend to favor adversarial commerce more than other industries. This business practice does not seem to be as prevalent to the same refined degree in other businesses, such as home building and construction. By contrasting these two vastly different industries, we can draw some empirical observations that help shed light on why adversarial commerce develops in one industry instead of another.

The auto industry is highly concentrated, with only 15 major global manufacturers remaining. The extremely high volume of production for these large firms also provides economies of scale. They produce millions of units of expensive product in relatively large centralized factories. Given the high degree of automation required in these plants, the companies are relatively locked into a fixed capacity that requires large amounts of capital to maintain. At least historically, each car company has vertically integrated many aspects of its production cycle and development by doing most of the elements within their own company rather than using outside suppliers. These large global companies continue to be highly integrated in their product-development systems and have fairly rigid and strong corporate cultures that feature heavy control mechanisms. Finally, they steadfastly hold on to the warranty of the finished unit for longer periods, to spread their control into the customers' extended use. This is an industry marked by consolidation and control over the market, as well as an industry in which the barriers to entry are significant.

Residential homebuilding seems to be at the opposite end of the spectrum. Although there are a few large national builders, such as Pulte or Kaufman Broad, this industry is still marked by significant decentralization and fragmentation. Each region and many cities have small local builders who, in cooperation with separate land developers, can still compete against the larger national firms. Interestingly, in contrast to automobiles, the housing industry has a large independent supplier community that develops its own products and promotes their use to a wide market. The annual volume of residential homes is impressively large in total, but the average output per builder is less than a hundred, compared to the millions of units per car assemblers. Home building is a large but nonintegrated industry involving literally thousands of associated supplier firms. Finally, most builders offer only limited warranties and use the warranty system of the supplier-provided equipment, such as appliances, furnishings, or heating/cooling to resolve customer issues.

Common Elements

The following table contrasts these two industries and the elements we have identified:

Home Construction	Auto Manufacturers
Fragmented industry	Concentrated industry
Low volume	High volume
Decentralized manufacturing	Centralized global manufacturing
Primarily individual manufacturing	High capital factories
Nonintegrated	Highly vertically integrated
Many corporate cultures	Rigid strong cultures
Offload warranty	Retail warranty

When we compare these industries, we begin to see some elements that, when present in a specific industry, might create an atmosphere that encourages adversarial tendencies to take hold. We see that highly concentrated and consolidated industries that have strong, well-established cultures coupled with a highly integrated internal manufacturing system can become very adversarial. Industries such as home building appear to be so fragmented that they cannot exhibit the same degree of leverage over their extended enterprise and are less adversarial because they rely more on the standard practices of commerce. One industry seems deeply set in negative dictatorial ways, and the other operates under more normal commercial rules of engagement.

The idea is that centralization of power within an industry might "taint" management behavior and make it easier for them to use their economic clout in a dictatorial and heavy-handed manner. Clearly, this is the prevailing case in current U.S. automobile management.

Testing the Premise

Let's now test this idea on some economic history in the United States. A list of industries with conditions similar to those of the auto industry might include the following:

Steel

Banking

Retailing

Publishing

Rubber

Agricultural equipment

Heavy truck

Entertainment (film/cable)

Commercial aerospace

Each of the industries has characteristics similar to those we identified earlier. As a group, these industries also are older, mature, and, in some cases, in the decline phase of their life cycle. They have gone through periods of rapid growth followed by overcapacity. An additional observation is that as these industries went through consolidation, reducing the number of companies involved, the remaining companies moved from being classified as "winners" to eventually and more accurately being called "survivors." During this rationalization phase, the individual companies were forced to hunker down and defend their remaining turf against other forms of competition. In doing so, they often became more defensive in their attitudes and sometimes more adversarial.

Each of these industries was a major employer that supported both lower-level assembly or service jobs and significant middle-management white-collar professionals. In many ways, this list represents the economic power that drove this country to prosperity after World War II. Now many of these represent much smaller aspects of our national economy in the twenty-first century.

Whether it was Firestone taking on its unions, banks charging customers to use their own ATM cards, U.S. Steel fighting against the smaller mini-mills, Kmart responding to Wal-Mart's aggressiveness by whipping suppliers, or airlines stranding their customers, adversarial commerce is commonly practiced in these separate and distinct industries. It does not just occur in the demented minds of Detroit businessmen; it can happen in any town, to any firm and almost any maturing industry.

Middle-Age Spread and Isolation

Another observation is that older, established companies are more inclined to fall into the adversarial trap than newer firms. This assumption can be explained by the fact an established culture tries many means to defend itself and make itself independent from others. As a firm ages, the bureaucratic aspects of the organization feed on this quest for independence. This action could make trusting extended partners more difficult.

It might begin with a firm establishing a negative attitude toward outside suppliers while trying to defend and maintain internal manufacturing or service. Often loyalty and self-pride make objective comparisons to outside parties a difficult thing to accomplish. After all, shouldn't a company trust its own employees above outsiders? Not always, and certainly not blindly. Time after time, while running Chrysler's component-manufacturing division, I had to listen to complaints about how unfair and evil our outside competitors were. Because of the size of the auto component industry, there was at least one strong independent supplier in every one of our component categories. The inside division was constantly being compared to these outside companies. This attitude helped the manufacturing people boost their feelings of self-worth, but it also blinded them to the realities that other firms might have been superior.

The negative tone toward suppliers can spread to other partners as well. Instead of treating unionized employees as true joint members in the firm, the U.S. automakers developed a very negative general attitude toward their UAW workforce. Over time, this opinion colored the fabric of each company's relationship as the management tended to mistrust the union and began to drive a wedge between the two sides that further complicated the quest to be competitive.

Beyond suppliers and unions, the attitude of "us against the world" was reflected in the automakers feelings toward their own dealers. The auto retailing system uses independent dealers to move the product. This relationship has often been one of antagonism instead of partnership. Ford upset its entire dealer franchise in the 1990s by experimenting in buying up independent dealers in certain markets, supposedly for better control of quality and service and perhaps pricing. Ford expended large sums to conduct this experiment in several locations, including Kansas City, where they attempted to buy all the independent dealers in town. They stopped when their national dealer network threatened revolution. The dealers felt let down by Ford's adversarial practices. This was yet another policy in which the dominant party tried to force a policy upon a larger but more fragmented group. In this case, however, the use of adversarial power failed because the economic cost was too high. The idea never was workable because there were just too many dealers to buy out to do a national program, and the capital required would have drained Ford's ability to develop new products. The dealer body banded together to resist the effort, but the attempt created deep feelings of mistrust instead of increasing sales.

These examples show how arrogance and the self-pride generated by an overriding need to exercise control can negatively influence the very relationships that a company must have to survive and grow. This inward-thinking orientation and defensive attitude has poisoned the ability of the U.S. automakers to react to change and has seriously endangered their very survival in the future.

The Spiral of Costs

Earlier chapters pointed out that one thing wrong with using adversarial commerce is that it actually increases costs over the long run. The financial area of an aggressive firm usually doesn't accept this fact, which makes it difficult to implement change. Increased costs over time can more than offset temporary short-run reductions that might be achieved. But the existing system of quarterly reporting to Wall Street keeps the overall focus on the short term. This short-run focus is also a result of the inward bias that exists in organizations that practice adversarial commerce routinely.

The result of constantly focusing inwardly is the generation of internal costs. As a company vertically integrates or protects those things it does to a fault, it might refuse to accept other approaches that actually would be more efficient. To offset these internal inefficiencies, the companies turn against the remaining outside parties with a greater degree of negativism. The management attitude becomes overly focused on the cost control side of the equation instead of revenue generation.

Suppliers are pressed for immediate reductions, but the results are not fast enough to combat the rising internal costs. Eventually, drastic cuts must be taken by laying off salaried and hourly personnel to get back into profitability. Wall Street and institutional investors often encourage this "slash and burn" approach. However, the danger is that concentrating on inward negative thinking creates a downward spiral as the company gets smaller and has higher costs, which, in turn, generates even more reduction actions and forces the firm to take less risk and implement less innovation. The company becomes conservative and might sacrifice its future plans as it tries to stay alive. This all leads to the company's eventual decline and stagnation, as has happened to many firms that were once leaders in the old-line industries we cited previously.

The tendency to try to solve the cost problem with harsh internal actions instead of seeking collaborative help also identifies companies deep into adversarial management. Instead of using the leverage of working with outside partners to reduce capital, internally focused development increases capital requirements. The internal capital costs increase and become too great of a burden to maintain leadership positions in competitive industries. The Big Three's actions mentioned earlier—the demand for arbitrary cost reductions and threats of canceling contracts with no warning—all create more suspicions in the minds of their suppliers about their ability to trust clients. This is all happening at the very time the company could be reducing the OEM's capital requirement by working on joint development and jointly sharing the costs that are saved. By the time the U.S. automakers wake up, the industry likely will have been permanently harmed by their use of adversarial methods.

Adversarial Commerce in R&D

One area of cost that increases under adversarial commerce is research and development. The tendency to do everything internally, out of either pride or a false sense of security, can greatly impact the cost of developing new products. This occurs in many companies, and an example from MSX can illustrate how it happens.

MSX International provides consolidated administrative and payment functions for companies to manage their temporary employment needs. This service is called Master Vendor Provider and is fairly common in the staffing industry. When we acquired a company in 1997, we inherited software to perform this function. At the time, it was unique and very customized. Over time, however, other software providers began to develop similar commercial systems. We actually purchased one of those competing programs as an effort to expand our product offerings.

The problem was that members of our own staffing division believed their own internally developed version was superior. They spent several million dollars to modify and upgrade our old system instead of working with the outside license holder to adapt his program to our needs. When it was all finished and presented to senior management for demonstration,

Adversarial Commerce in R&D

it became clear that our own system had no inherent advantage over the commercially available one. We had spent a considerable amount of development money that could have been avoided by working with the outside licensee at less cost and time. Why did this happen? Our internal division wanted to avoid working with anyone outside, and we mainly believed that no one else could develop anything equal to what we could do.

The development of this customized unique system was justified as keeping our proprietary software advantage. But the staffing division spent capital that could have been better directed to other more profitable areas of the company. That expenditure actually reduced the profitability of the business instead of improving it because MSX could not charge the customers for the development cost. It was our own employees' fear of collaboration and desire to do everything internally that hurt MSX, just as it has in many other companies.

The short-term concentration that occupies management when it uses negative relations minimizes the company's ability to prepare for the future. Shortcutting or limiting research and development efforts saps the life out of a company because no firm can continue to sell the same product forever. Clearly, one of management's most difficult tasks is to properly balance short-term financial results with the longer-term investments needed to grow the firm. Under collaborative management, leveraging development with partner companies is one way to reduce this expense. A reputation of trust, stability, and evenhandedness is needed to approach partners effectively. Companies that mistrust suppliers or treat suppliers, dealers, or customers poorly will not find it easy to add a new development partner under acceptable terms.

When the behavior of a firm becomes characterized as negative or adversarial, the companies that deal with that firm become cautious. Too often management assumes that economic leverage or power can force related firms into following the firm's demands. As the industrial world becomes more global, suppliers and customers have more choices and our old system of economic pressures might have to be revised.

Not Just Autos

As we described, there are predictable situations in which negative management tactics seem to take over in companies. The examples we used were often oriented toward the automotive industry because it is the largest industry that currently is practicing intentionally adversarial methods. But the danger of companies resorting to these harsh tactics exists everywhere in U.S. commerce. These examples highlight a few areas in which the practice is not limited to the past or just to suppliers, but to other partners. The premise that firms get further into trouble by resorting to negative practices shows up in the major airlines, which neglected their customers and opened the door to new competition; in the U.S. steel industry, which used trade protectionism to mask their lack of competitiveness; in the banking industry, which saw many companies exit retail banking because it looked too unprofitable to respond to customer complaints of bad service; and in retailing, in which Wal-Mart uses its economic clout to dictate terms to its suppliers.

Certainly, the economic failings of the industries and companies used in these examples are not just the result of using adversarial commerce tactics. Many other internal or external factors have contributed to these situations. The point is that, in many of them, the old-style command and control management philosophy probably helped accelerate their decline or limited recovery. The practice is widespread and growing as management often continues to use the "follow the leader" approach by copying what is done in other industries. The next chapter examines a common trait that is practiced almost universally: the control of information.

Endnotes

1. Lucette Lagnado, *Wall Street Journal* "Hospitals Try Extreme Measures," 30 October 2003, pg 1.

5

INFORMATION IS POWER AND SHARING DOESN'T COME NATURALLY

An army might run on its stomach, but the business world runs on information. Knowledge of the internal and external happenings of the firm is essential to any effective manager. The more information you have, the better, and the more private and sensitive it is, the more useful it is to you. These truths might seem obvious, but it is important to recognize the manner in which we use the information that we have and the extremes we go to in order to protect it. If we want to change our existing commercial system, we must look at information flow and speed, especially as the growth of the web-based communication has increased both the amount and access to data. Our ability to communicate has greatly improved, but what we do with the information is still largely based on tradition. Our management techniques have not caught up with the advancements in technology. If we are to expand our way of management into a more collaborative manner, we need to expand communication and the way in which we use and share it.

As organizations build their hierarchical structures, they often build in a process that protects the information within a department or division. This capture and protection of data sometimes goes so far as to require specific management approval before data is shared even within other areas of the firm.[1] We are all familiar with examples in which sales managers of a firm don't want results released to senior management until they have fully reviewed them, or the engineering manager does not let the cost status of his project be known until he is ready to release it. These are understandable actions usually based on the fact that management previously quizzed or challenged the manager on the results before he had a chance to analyze the data. Good managers know that they need to have explanations ready to defend results. But sometimes this protection of data is based on the negative desire to keep the status of something confidential as long as possible so that management has little choice but to accept the bad news when it is delivered. The control of business information has many aspects.

Most companies have hundreds of different sources and many different sets of information. There are formal information bases, such as the financial system that summarizes and reports the profit and loss results, the operational system that measures performance and is used to run the daily business, and the human resources systems that track the employment issues and compensation, to highlight just a few.

These formal systems can become quite institutionalized and rigid. They have developed over years and usually function well; sometimes they are seen as the only solution. Newly acquired companies are often forced to modify their financial and operational systems to conform to those of the new owner. That makes data collection easier for the parent company but could interrupt or add costs to the newly acquired entity. Although separate data systems can be accommodated, their existence often is an annoyance for the larger firm, which might use its new ownership control to force a common way. New regulations required under the Sarbanes/Oxley Act seem to be pushing companies into more conformity, to comply with the laws.

Any organization also has a vast network of informal information sources, whether town hall discussions with employees, one-on-one sessions with subordinates, or the word-of-mouth rumors that circulate through any workplace. Often these sources produce incorrect or partial information that is sometimes given creditability equal to that coming from the formal system. These factoid-based items are often used by management in what can be labeled as "vignette management"—that is, the tendency to value information that is anecdotal and often unsupported by research data. This is helped by the fact that the informal commerce system usually works faster than the more accurate formal system.

These informal information systems are much more important than many managers realize. The rumor mill is not only fast, but very accurate in its tone, if not in its detailing of facts. Ignoring rumors or avoiding the use of informal data sources is a dangerous practice.

How management uses these various formal and informal sets of information is a function of the culture, tradition, and organization of a company. The data can be used proactively to head off problems or can be used reactively to respond to situations after they develop. The best answer is to use information for both situations, but too often the pressure of daily business and an over-reliance on the accounting system lead companies into reactive instead of proactive mode.

I once had a supervisor whose personal and professional motto was " I don't need a strategy. My strategy is to wait to see what happens and then to react faster than anyone else." It always bothered me that this guy seemed so nonstrategic and didn't want to spend time planning where he wanted to take the organization. Under his leadership, we were guided by outside influences instead of our own ideas. Yet, in the firm where we both worked, that reactive nature reflected the company culture. The whole information system was geared toward measuring what was going on and then responding or making adjustments, not analyzing the information to come up with new directions or anticipating change.

Many companies use this "follow-the-leader" approach. It can actually be effective in the short run, but it can't maintain growth over time. In many industries, there are examples of executives who having proposed following the market leader and copying their actions. The automotive, computer, retailing, and entertainment industries are prime examples. But whether it was Chrysler following Ford, Compac following Dell, Kmart following Wal-Mart, or CBS following NBC, companies that rely on an information flow that just monitors the current situation and isn't analyzed for the future seem to get into trouble eventually.

The Dreaded Finance Staff

One result of the evolution of our commercial system is that large corporations have institutionalized information gathering into functional areas. Groups such as finance, human resources, and legal are examples of activities within companies that are chartered with providing the professional oversight of the type of data they control. This is done to provide consistent application across the company. One of the worst examples is the financial system. Recent accounting scandals and the resultant reforms could compound this problem in the future. Companies necessarily have needed to centralize financial reporting to meet the demands of various regulatory and tax authorities. Under the new regulations, each quarter the CFO and CEO of any public company (or private company with public debt) must now sign formal certifications of accuracy as part of their 10Q and annual 10K filing with the SEC. Now these individuals are personally obligated to vouch for the accuracy of the data; they can't hide behind an accountant to blame. The system that produces the data to allow such certifications has suddenly become even more important than it was previously.

The responsibility for all this usually falls on the finance activity within a firm. The growth in the accounting and financial control areas of a firm parallels the company's overall growth pattern. These financial areas derive their authority from the specialized nature of what they do. The CPAs, CFAs, and MBAs that populate the finance areas of the companies isolate these areas from other levels in the company. This fact, coupled with the necessary nature of controlling the reporting system, gives those in the financial group a great deal of formal and informal authority. Again, the issue is how the finance department uses the information it has, not the fact that it exists.

Many companies are organized around unique product lines or businesses. These business units usually have their own controller and finance group, which also report directly into a central finance function. Accordingly, the finance community has unique access to the entire firm, whereas each business leader sees only his own portion. This permits each division or unit to concentrate on its own performance, but it also means that only the CFO knows how the total company is doing. The data and information that is transmitted up through this system sometimes gets manipulated and adjusted by the central staff as it rolls into the final corporate number. If this practice is used too frequently and too extensively, the operating people have a hard time seeing the total results of their efforts.

This happened in my own company with our financial forecasts. When I arrived at MSX International as CEO after leaving DaimlerChrysler, I found that MSX was tightly controlled by its financial system. All forecasts were prepared by the finance people within a business unit and were sent to the controller and finally to the CFO before they were shared with the operational head of the unit. No real-time data was available to the managers, so they had to wait each month for the central staff to gather, massage, filter, and overlay the results. There was even a practice of withholding distribution of the internal results until the CEO and CFO sent them to the outside owners/investors for review. As a result, the operating management was both left in the dark and isolated from the results. Managers had come to feel less responsible for their actions because they did not have a voice in preparing the forecast or know about the results until after they were rolled. It was a bad situation that worsened when our company, MSX, ran into reduced revenue and profits as a result of the automotive downturn in 2002 and 2003. Terminating this process was extremely difficult because of the long-standing formal and informal power of the finance organization in the company. With the central finance staff massaging and adjusting the information, the operating areas did not feel as if they owned their own forecasts, nor did they feel responsible for meeting them. It took several management changes to finally get the system more open and transparent. Now we can see the same data at the same time the managers see it and can hold people accountable for their actions.

The danger lurking in this process is the lack of information sharing. MSX followed the old adage of "the less you know, the better." Over time, the reporting system took on a life of its own. The measures or reports generated had little to do with operating the businesses we were running. At times, we were measuring things that really didn't matter, wasting time and effort that could have been spent concentrating on managing the business instead of just reporting on it. In addition, the finance organization was the single control point for passing on information. Over time, this type of overcontrol can isolate the business leaders from what is going on and reduce their accountability. This is one of the organizational problems of trying to run a company in multiple business lines and regions.

We encountered similar information-sharing problems during the formation of DaimlerChrysler. The new company was required to be organized under German laws, which involved having a supervisory board (which closely resembled an American company's board of directors) and a separate management board that included the major senior operating executives. The management board made most of the tactical decisions and ran the daily operations of the global company. It met regularly to review the vast and diversified operations of the new company, nicknamed DCX.

The communication problems began because we maintained two separate headquarters: the German one from Daimler in Stuttgart, and the American one from Chrysler in Detroit. The agenda and coordination of all reports and documents discussed in the management board were centralized under a planning area in Stuttgart. Because all the Daimler members were relatively close in Germany, it was easy for them to get the information and review it before meetings. With our distant location in Detroit, the Chrysler side initially received the materials just before leaving for overnight flights to Germany. Whether intentional or not, the result was that the Daimler side often had more familiarity with the subjects than did the Chrysler executives. To equalize this situation, the American side established a small coordination unit to help facilitate communication and information sharing. This ended up with a major confrontation between the Daimler representatives and their American counterparts, with angry accusations of power grabbing hurled against the Americans. Apparently, who controlled the information and how it was handled was a sensitive topic in the German business culture. We were accused of trying to "block vote" by having our own area coordinate information for us. Eventually, the conflict was resolved, but not until there was direct involvement between Juergen Schrempp and myself. We had to promise not to have prior reviews to develop a common position, just as we had suspected the German side was doing. For months I was licking my wounds from this attempt to solve a problem.

One of our greatest battles during the initial years of DaimlerChrysler involved confusion over the measurement of cash. Because of its previous periods of financial difficulty, Chrysler had an accurate and fast information system that produced a cash statement after each month of operation. It also helped that we were in a single line of business, so the data could be collected centrally. Daimler-Benz, on the other hand, was extremely decentralized and had to roll up its cash statements from many separate units and groups spread across the world. Under German reporting rules, they were much less concerned about the cash usage and forecasting than Chrysler had been.

Our first three management board meetings were almost comical when we reached discussions on reporting our cash status. When the newly merged companies' CFO was asked to produce a cash statement, he replied it would take a while to develop. The Chrysler side pressed him to develop one for the next month's meeting showing in detail the source and use of the cash. The next meeting came, and the result was the same very general, macro-level summary used at Daimler-Benz. When again questioned about the detail, the CFO dismissed the concept of revealing more detail to the board members. His comment was essentially, "You have enough, and that's all that you need to know."

To resolve this problem, the previous Chrysler assistant controller, Jim Donlon, was assigned to Stuttgart from Detroit to show the German side how to count cash the way Wall Street analysts require it to be done. This created enormous friction between the two financial activities of the company and was another of our long-standing implementation differences that took too much time to properly resolve.

The problem in the DaimlerChrysler situation was not the lack of a proper accounting system to measure the operational cash requirements. Both companies had adequate systems. The real issue was the fact that the data was now required to be shared with the larger new board. The Chrysler members subjected the CFO to questions he had never had to answer previously in front of his fellow peers. He was against sharing it and against having his responses challenged. He derived much of his power in the CFO position by possessing data that no one else had. He was reluctant to share the information because he felt he would lose both influence and control. This situation represented much of the difficulties we experienced in our first year as a mega-merger company.

Staff Versus Line Reporting

The power that the financial side of an organization has over the various internal functions being measured can be enormous. It happens in small companies such as MSX and large ones such as DaimlerChrysler or Ford in the 1970s. When I worked at Ford, its finance staff prided itself in its elite status, while, at the same time, its staff members were widely negatively referred to within the company. Their control went to such lengths that the CFO at the time, Ed Lundy, even published an internal dictionary of acceptable phrases and terms to be used in finance memos. The information gathered from the units was distilled into one common, very controlled language. On one hand, it seemed to work well, in that the finance activity had its finger on the pulse of the company. On the other hand, it operated very independently and was never considered part of the operating team. For this reason, most of the organization viewed it with great suspicion and fear. Some people call this creating necessary "tension" in the system, but it can also inhibit communication and prompt disclosure of problems.

Usually, these strong finance activities are organized by staff groups, independent from the operating management. The idea is for them to be a separate set of eyes and ears for the senior management to use to check up on the real business. This checks and balances system can help if the operating people understand it and have not been conditioned to "game" the system. But the existence of a strong central and independent finance staff can turn ugly when it starts developing or recommending strategies without consulting the line groups. This can lead to a lack of trust in the organization, hampering the commercial enterprise and leading to adversarial commerce both internally and externally. It is also extremely inefficient for CEOs to feel that they must look to a staff reporting or analysis group to verify what their operating heads are telling them. But this is exactly the case in many companies where adversarial commerce has been allowed to become the culture.

Internally, this kind of practice places the staff in opposition to the line activities, creating unnecessary tension and information shielding. Fear of having facts used against them by senior management is a main reason mistrust can build within a company. Externally, it can be even more damaging because mistrust can be created among the outside partners necessary for operation. As noted earlier, the current system of commerce has evolved to the state in which firms religiously protect their independent status and their operating information. Information sharing with external partners is resisted in tightly controlled firms. A couple examples highlight how companies seldom discriminate between their valued supplier and their competition.

In the automotive industry, sales are reported on a monthly basis. They are published by the industry press in detail by manufacturer, brand, nameplate, and, in many cases, individual model. In addition, the stocks of finished vehicles awaiting sales on dealer lots are published in the same detail. Everyone knows what is selling and what's not, and how many units are stacking up at the dealers. There is little to hide. Unfortunately, the manufacturing system operates not on this actual sales data, but on the projections the auto companies send weekly. These forecasts, or material releases, are the legal commitment that each company makes to order parts and services for the next period of production, which normally runs the following 30 to 60 days. Adjustments can be made weekly but are rarely changed until it becomes too late.

A supplier can see the real sales results, but often the public manufacturing plan runs opposite to the historic sales trend. From the first shipment on a contract, the Big Three warn suppliers to only follow the release and never second-guess the lofty car companies. The car companies are reluctant to make cuts because of the complexity of the process and the fact that their financial forecasts to Wall Street are set months ahead of time. It all works well when sales are hot and inventory is not building. When demand starts to fall, a curious dilemma starts.

The supplier, which has access to the public sales data like everyone else and who sees the sales dropping, has to decide whether to believe his client's schedule or to discount it. As an independent business, it does not want to be left holding inventory. Because demand is dropping, the car companies will have to address the issue. They could either cut production or increase the sales incentives offered. If they increase the incentives, the production schedule will hold. If they cut production, suppliers could be left with raw and semifinished material for which they would not be immediately paid. What to do?

The answer is that most suppliers automatically discount the releases independently of what the Big Three actually forecast. They take a risk that the volume won't happen, and if it does go up, they can order more material at a small penalty. They have learned over time that they are better off not trusting the auto companies' planning because they have often been left holding the bag. They have learned that the Big Three can delay resolution of inventory disputes to manage cash. The U.S. Big Three have traditionally established production schedules that fluctuate much more than the Japanese or other foreign makers. As a result, the cost of doing business with the U.S. domestic automakers is higher for suppliers than it is when doing business with foreign transplants. This higher cost is passed on to the U.S. automakers, further hurting their competitive position. Our commercial system once again has been modified and corrected by new arrivals, and our older companies are too slow to change.

It also happens in the advanced production phase of engineering and design. Most people in the industry who follow car design remarked how controversial the Pontiac Aztec vehicle looked when it was first revealed to them at the Detroit Auto Show. General Motors was telling its supply base to tool and protect for an annual production volume of more than 200,000 of these odd-looking things. The actual sales in the first year fell to less than half that number. Most suppliers discounted the GM plans and did not bother to reserve the total capacity that they were asked to do. Again, because of a lack of shared information, they were forced into a situation in which they had to either protect themselves or believe the larger company. Recent history seems to indicate that a supplier should never believe the optimism that is contained in the domestic auto industry playbook. The result has been a loosely played game in which the suppliers no longer can trust the major manufacturers to give them accurate data for planning purposes. The current system is operating as if the players all have secretly modified the rules in favor of themselves. The overprotection of information that could be shared without creating difficulties is the heart of the problem.

Risk Sharing Must Be Fact Based

The Big Three senior leaders are all currently begging suppliers to trust them and to help them in their difficult task of regaining market share and profitability. The problem is that, through years of managing the information flow to filter out facts, it is increasingly hard for anyone to believe them. When challenged to explain the situation, the U.S. automakers often resort to the time-tested line that business is based on taking risks and that suppliers, dealers, and other related firms must share in that risk with them. That makes fine sense and is the nature of most successful business relationships. The problem here is that, to be equitable, the decision to take these financial risks must be based on shared information. Otherwise, the decision is made in a vacuum. Trust can be created by sharing information such as future plans, sales forecasts, and sales plans so that each party operates from the same level of understanding and the same set of facts. In that way, if the involved parties all realize that a new design is controversial, they can plan more efficiently to protect themselves for both the upside and the downside in production. The current system is based on the odd belief that everything that is planned and communicated by the vehicle manufacturers will happen with certainty. In reality, it rarely does.

Again, we should not pick solely on the auto industry. This lack of information sharing exists in most industries. As noted in Chapter 4, the retailing industry is similar to the automotive industry because retailers did not see the value of direct sharing of information. Wal-Mart is an outstanding example of a company that recognized the value of letting its suppliers directly see the daily sales data and letting them be responsible for managing many aspects of their supply chain. Other retailers have tried to catch Wal-Mart, but its advantage of data use and its leverage has enabled Wal-Mart to become the largest retailer in the world and to drive competitors (such as Kmart) either out of business or into Chapter 11.

The previous chapter detailed how Kmart did not have a competitive information system. Instead of spending the time and money to develop it, the company launched into a disastrous discounting program, basically blind to how it was working.

Certainly, a large amount of data and information within a company is proprietary and must remain within the firm. The idea to share more data with outside companies does not mean that sensitive information should be distributed. Every company must form its own strategy and develop its own plans. The problem is that the culture of many companies has evolved so that management considers *all* information to be confidential. This practice leads to continued separation between companies that could be acting more as partners than as enemies. Control of information and a lack of information sharing are the worst elements that have developed in the system of adversarial commerce. We need to throw out the old model of protection and look for ways to collaborate and yet retain the data that is the heart and soul of a company.

The Solution: More Transparent Information

The answer to the problem of one group or company using information to control another is to adopt a system that is much more transparent. Transparency means that the information is actual and does not require filtering or adjustment before it can be used. It is available at the same time that it is collected, and can be viewed by parties at several levels, from the operating floor to the CEO, and by both line and staff organizations. All parties use the same information, with access controlled only by the need to protect company confidentiality.

Under a collaborative system, the information used is both transparent and two-way. The tendency in adversarial commerce is to control the downward flow and to limit the information transmitted to only the minimum amount necessary for employees or suppliers to perform their specific tasks. Upward information flow to the primary or dominant company is not encouraged, or if it is received, it is often ignored. Two-way communication permits the suppliers performing their jobs to communicate back to their clients. They can advise them of problems in meeting schedules, offer alternative suggestions for cost or timing, or provide market information that is unavailable to the client. This information sharing in a mutual manner fosters interdependence and facilitates better responses to change in the business environment. It sounds simple to trust information from a worker or supplier, but for many firms operating under an adversarial style, it threatens their control and domination. For that very reason, companies looking to extend collaboration must vigilantly insist on using faster, two-way transparent data as the language of communication.

Opening the communication channels can reduce costs by making the supply chain leaner. This reduces inventories and can avoid the expense of sudden and drastic changes to the production schedule. This is the nature of the Japanese Kan-Ban system for smooth manufacturing throughout the chain. But when the data is enlarged to include planning and forecasting information, it means giving up some control. Previously, the company might have justified not sharing this because it was viewed as proprietary to its operation. In reality, there is much less secret information than companies believe should exist, and much of what might be confidential can actually be shared with the appropriate level of management in other companies after rules and trust have been established.

These rules would govern the use of data, define who receives it and is personally responsible for it, and establish penalties for its misuse. Admittedly, a greater sharing of information between companies exposes both to greater mutual risk. But these risks seem to be small when compared to the advantages of open communication. The risks are often overplayed and used as an excuse not to share data or embrace change. Sharing does not mean revealing secrets; it merely means providing more relevant information that can help the chain understand conditions and anticipate problems.

So far, we have spent some time and detail defining what is wrong with the current adversarial system and how prevalent it is in our economy. The remainder of this book offers a more optimistic alternative and shows how that negative system can be changed for the betterment of all parties. The answer is in expanded use of collaboration to break out of the cycle we find ourselves in presently.

Endnotes

1. The prevailing business analysis term for one of these in a company is a silo.

6

THE COLLABORATIVE
APPROACH

Comfort in Using Traditional Tactics

Managers struggle constantly with unknowns as they adjust to varied and shifting commercial environments. As global competition increases, American businessmen and businesswomen will need different tactics than they have used in the past to make adjustments more quickly. Just following the curve or copying the accepted norm will not take a company to the higher levels required to stay ahead of that new competition. But following the old rules, or taking the standard traditional response, is often exactly the course managers choose because it is comfortable and subject to less criticism. Breaking out of the pack of standardized actions and attempting to do something different is often viewed as more risky than just muddling through during a down period.

The traditional management response during periods of financial pressure is to restructure to reduce bloated overheads that were built up during more profitable times, and to reduce the workforce to adjust to periods of slower demand for products. If those don't work or the owners get impatient, management can always be replaced. During the slow economy in the early years of this millennium, use of these traditional measures increased, but it is not clear whether they really resulted in anything other than occupying time until the general economy improved. It is often hard to tell whether a company recovers because of restructuring or whether it just waited enough time for the external conditions to improve. There was little evidence that innovative management approaches were taken during that period of relative financial stress.

This illustrates the danger that, as we evolve and modify our traditional management practices, some companies have adopted a style that fits the definition of adversarial commerce. Instead of working more closely with other firms, they tend to become more insulated and hostile to the very firms they need to help produce their product or service.

What seems to be apparent is the need for an alternative set of tactics that can make a firm more nimble, faster, and more efficient. The premise of this book is that companies need to look at the way they interface with other companies necessary for their success and must modify the standard approach previously used to manage them. By adopting more collaborative techniques, they can tap into the power, resources, and energy of those companies they utilize without having to resort to acquisition.

Acquisition Is the Easy Way Out

Historically, when the management of one firm realizes that another company has become critical to its own survival or expansion, the traditional approach is to look to acquire the other company. Acquisition is part of the fabric of our economy, pushed by investment bankers and worn like a badge of honor on the chests of executives. It is easier and faster, and it satisfies our deep-seated desire for control. It also makes CEOs feel as if they have taken a bold step that can jump-start their own company, if not their career. It seems that acquiring related firms just makes management feel like they won a contest or a battle and have cleared the decks for another period.

During the last decade, the level of mergers and acquisitions (M&A) accelerated to record paces, peaking with the more than $1,325 billion spent on acquisitions in the year 2000 alone. That level fell off because of the softer economies of the subsequent two or three years, but it is again on the upswing as earnings and conditions improve.

Why does management often resort to acquisition as the preferred method of growth? In addition to satisfying the competitive instinct to control an environment, it is quick. It can instantly increase both sales and profits and provide some synergy in savings by reducing newly combined common activities. Based on the level of M&A in the recent past, this clearly is the accepted tactic to use. Unfortunately, studies have shown that most mergers and many acquisitions fail to increase value for the shareholders of the acquiring company.

When we were preparing for the merger of Chrysler and Daimler-Benz in 1998, the investment bankers on both sides, Goldman Sachs and Credit Suisse First Boston, each advised their respective clients that, based on their own research, more than 75 percent of mergers done in the 1990s did not live up to their published objectives to create growth or value for their shareholders. Other studies have verified this fact. Managers get caught up in the mood of the moment and the emotion of the deal and believe, as we did in our case, that they are in a unique situation. They ignore history and continue to proceed to acquire companies without sufficiently exploring any other alternatives. Partnerships and alliances are not in favor because they are nontraditional and have been generally viewed as too difficult to control.

Although it is popular, management's fascination with acquiring can also be expensive in both financial and strategic sense. It can sap a company of its management attention and focus. The newly acquired company's previous management might not come along into the new firm, either because they were bought out or because the acquiring company did not consider them necessary. These defectors could entice other critical talent that had not been identified in the due diligence period to leave with them. This further destroys the value of the targeted firm. If the original managers stay, they might not fit in with the acquirer's culture or style.

Collaboration Defined

The alternative approach to the adversarial tactics common in today's economy is for firms to encourage closer collaboration between them. Instead of acquisition, managers can utilize alliances to obtain the same desired result of growth in revenue and profit with less risk. Instead of browbeating suppliers into submission to reduce prices, initiating joint cost-sharing programs can yield even greater results. Whether they use alliances, cost sharing, joint ventures, or consortiums, they all fall under the broader term of collaboration. For our purposes, collaboration is any management practice that features close and organized or managed cooperation between independent firms. This attitude of cooperation involves participative planning to achieve a desired specific purpose. The main feature of a collaborative system that distinguishes it from the negative dictatorial command method is that here the involved parties work jointly as a common team, with each member being responsible for an assigned role.

Instead of being dictatorial by assigning arbitrary tasks or targets, a collaborative atmosphere allows for discussion and the exchange of ideas. This should not be misinterpreted as being without control or the ability to be managed. Managed collaboration describes the process in which a firm takes a leadership role in facilitating the cooperation between subordinate firms that normally would be mere suppliers of good or services. A company can embrace the principles of collaboration and still remain in as much direct control as it did under the command and dictate system. It just requires planning, commitment to make it work, and involved leadership.

A successful collaboration project features several unique elements that are missing from the more traditional management structures we have discussed earlier. These are the primary ones:

1. Sense of partnership and shared interests

2. Shared goals and rewards

3. Open and unfiltered lines of communication

4. Clear definition of the roles and responsibilities

5. Freedom to make necessary decisions within the scope of responsibility

Each of these elements must be present and active in a truly collaborative relationship to permit the work on the project to be streamlined and apportioned. First, the parties must respect that they enter into the agreement as partners, not as in the feudal master/serf relationship. They must also agree and see the opportunity for both sides to profit in the successful completion of the work, with each side assuming some degree of risk that is proportional to their gain. If the risk is perceived to be too uneven or one-sided, that party will create ways to reduce it by potentially building protection mechanisms into its responses. Those actions would reduce the cooperation and inhibit the early resolution of problems and opportunities. The need for clearly defined roles helps each side understand its responsibilities in the project. Finally, each party must agree that if it accepts its defined role, it has a large degree of freedom to decide how to accomplish the task that is required.

A Call for Collaboration

Calling for closer cooperation between companies might sound too idealistic and naïve for aggressive companies to undertake. However, there is a movement beginning in business to push for alliances between companies to provide an alternative to the problems with the acquisition model mentioned earlier. Computer equipment, pharmaceutical makers, and others have shown that working jointly with a supplier or a closely related firm on development and production can help them achieve a competitive advantage. Dell, Intel, and similar innovative companies are seeing the benefits of collaboration, including reduced capital, access to more technologies, reduced permanent commitment, and faster speed to market.

In their book *The American Keiretsu*,[1] authors David N. Burt and Michael F. Doyle show how Japanese companies have a strategic advantage in their closely held Keiretsu style of management. The Keiretsu approach uses vertically aligned companies with separate but closely tied managements to work jointly on common programs. Often the companies trade both executives and workers, and offer management positions for retired executives from the other firm. This is the way Toyota began its working relationships with Denso (then named Nippondenso) and Aishin Seiki. These companies make the climate-control systems and transmissions, respectively, for Toyota. At one time, Toyota had direct ownership of these two companies, but, through time, they have evolved into completely separate structures. But their heritage and commitment to their former parent remains strong. Denso and Seiki now have other automakers as their customers, but their operation with Toyota remains seamless and the most efficient. Instead of treating them as distant and independent entities, Toyota shares product planning and proprietary cost information with these two companies. Both companies assume complete responsibility for developing the components that they are assigned on a Toyota project. The engineers of the assembler (Toyota) and the component maker (Denso or Seiki) often work as joint team members in each other's facilities. Toyota controls the overall specifications and has the responsibility for the finished vehicle, of course. But Toyota trusts these suppliers to do the detailed work on important components to meet the development and production schedules. Working jointly and in such close cooperation with its own Keiretsu is one way that Toyota is able to leverage its development of new products and come to market more quickly than the domestic American automakers.

Each of the Japanese carmakers had at one time its own separate Keiretsu that supported the parent or dominant company. As the Japanese production system spread globally, some of the weaker manufacturers were forced to seek other suppliers in addition to their own established partners. This was more a matter of financial prudence than intent. If left alone, the successful Japanese companies such as Toyota and Honda would have kept this system. Instead, outside political pressures, primarily from the United States and European governments, helped reduce the dominance of the Keiretsu outside of Japan as these companies moved into new geographic markets.

The concept of close collaboration is actually an attempt to integrate the various pieces of the commercial system that have been kept isolated for so long. As shown in the beaver hat example of Chapter 2, "Adversarial Commerce and Why It's Wrong," our commercial trade and enterprise system is based on individually distinct elements that have rarely needed to share anything other than a product for a payment. Companies make their wares and sell them to another company, and it all happens very well on the surface. But this process can be vastly improved and streamlined if we take a lesson from other economies that have been built up through a different process.

The lesson to be learned from the Japanese is not in the organization of their Keiretsu system, but in the communication and tactics the system uses. The organizational structure is contrary to our American tradition of independence, in that it features interlocking directorships and subsidized capital investment. These specifically go against regulations put in place here after the turn of the twentieth century. The Keiretsu system has its faults in organization, but when studied closely, it offers a model to modify and apply to our own commercial enterprise in the United States. In particular, we can look at how separate firms are able to work in unison while maintaining their own identity and servicing other customers. Later in this book, you will consider the elements of how to build your own collaborative enterprise. This is just what we did at Chrysler in the 1990s.

The Extended Enterprise®

Our idea was to establish a closer relationship with our outside suppliers, to make Chrysler more competitive as we struggled against intense pressure from our traditional competitors and from the expanding threat from the Japanese. We had always defined our lives at Chrysler as having gone from one "near death" experience to another. It was a chain of ups and downs, with the successes just about equaling the falls. But we were survivors in an industry that had seen all but three manufacturers drop from the market. It seems that, just as in the life cycle of cicada insects, we would emerge about every ten years from a period of success only to enter a cycle of depression in which our economic existence was threatened. It happened in 1980 and again in 1990. You might say that it happened again in 2001 when the surviving entity within the new DaimlerChrysler once more announced a major loss and the resultant restructuring. But during the 1990s, we became the largest and must successful company using collaboration as a coordinated corporate strategy. It worked so well and made us so profitable that it was one of the major assets that made us attractive to Daimler-Benz to approach for a merger.

Upon reflection, the cycle of the automobile industry business ups and downs is not much different from that experienced by many other companies in other industries. Most heavy manufacturing industries, such as steel, housing, aerospace, and defense, seem to go through these boom-and-bust cycles. The cycles happen so often that we are taught that business cycles are natural and something that can't be avoided. They can occur like the tides or phases of the moon. Academics and stockbrokers alike have made careers on the market timing and the effects of these cycles. But when these cycles happen and you, as a manager, are in the middle of trying to decide who to lay off or which plant to close, the thought that others might have been there before you never seems to bring much solace. The only answer is getting through the problem and completing the cycle.

At Chrysler, we studied our Japanese competition. We actually had a long history working with our on-again, off-again partner, Mitsubishi Motors Corp. Chrysler had owned a large portion of Mitsubishi until we were forced to sell it off during one of our periods of financial retrenchment. Both companies jointly worked on product and distribution, and even built a joint venture (JV) plant in Bloomington/Normal, Illinois, which later was turned over entirely to Mitsubishi.

During this almost two-decade relationship, we saw just how the Keiretsu worked, although, because of Mitsubishi's own financial weakness, its relationships with suppliers were far from the Toyota model of efficiency. Still, it gave us some insight into another way for related parties to operate other than the adversarial system that then was in play in the domestic auto industry.

In addition to the Japanese, we studied what was happening in the U.S. computer industry. Massive changes were underway as old-line manufacturers such as IBM and Apple were going through their own financial and product restructuring. As mentioned previously, new upstarts such as Dell and Compac were grabbing market share and rapidly expanding their production. But the manufacturing methods of these relatively new companies were different. Instead of relying on internal manufacture of the major components, these companies were working with their suppliers to introduce a much simpler and faster supply chain. We looked closer and talked to companies such as Intel. Intel, a major supplier to Dell, was developing its own style of supply chain management that relied heavily on close relationships with other businesses to cut time to market for new products. We believed there was something happening that we could apply to ourselves and our situation at Chrysler. The innovative spin was based on finding new ways to communicate and relate to outside companies while still keeping the independence that was necessary and practical in our economy. Dell and Intel were truly working on a collaborative model that made our way of doing business in Detroit look Byzantine.

The premise behind our idea for collaboration was to play upon the fact that Chrysler and its suppliers were as closely linked in their joint destiny as the Japanese were with their own list of suppliers. We had a long history of relationships, although we managed them through the adversarial system that was the model in Detroit. Until Lopez arrived upon the scene at GM, all the companies in Detroit had followed the same manner of treating suppliers like serfs or something lower than dirt. It was very much like being in a military basic training program, in which the plebes or recruits are constantly reminded of the power and authority that their superior officers had over them. Independent thought and unauthorized conduct were discouraged. The system was run by the Big Three automakers, which were each chasing the other instead of looking at the foreign competition.

Eventually, we at Chrysler created a collaborative management philosophy that we termed our Extended Enterprise, in recognition that our business went far beyond the bounds of the walls of our assembly plants. Our goal was to create an integrated, seamless system that did much more than just pass parts from suppliers to our factories. It was a system that shared communications, product plans, and research concepts with those companies that we needed to operate in close cooperation with us. It stressed the shared destiny that our joint businesses brought together but had previously overlooked or ignored under the forced and harsh competition of adversarial management. In short, it was an open recognition that we needed our suppliers as much as they needed us.

Never before in such a large and established business had any company attempted to put such a system into reality and to do it while continuing to work in the same industrial environment as before. We were trying to change the rules, while the other domestic players, General Motors and Ford, were continuing to run by the old set of plays for their own businesses. It was truly a risky experiment, but, as detailed in later chapters, it not only worked— it revitalized the company. Simply stated, the Chrysler Extended Enterprise was one of the largest and most successful approaches to industrial collaboration undertaken at its time.

Collaboration Is More Than E-commerce

In the past few years, there has been a mushrooming of discussion and talk about how firms can use e-commerce to institute collaboration. This talk has been hyped beyond reality, and there have been many false starts and missteps. The essence of collaboration is based on faster, more direct, and more automatic transfer of information between companies. But the mere movement of data more rapidly between companies is not the issue. Collaboration is how each company uses that exchanged data to work toward similar goals and to assign tasks within a business project. Reliance on using the same data, some of which might have been considered proprietary in previous business cases, helps bring the management of the related companies closer together. It is sort of like "We are in this together, and there is no hiding." Except for related security aspects, it really doesn't matter how this data is communicated. It can be by electronic means or regular channels. What is important is that the data is shared, unfiltered, and accurate.

Around the beginning of this decade, there was a movement to introduce new Internet-based communication tools to various industries. Led by the aggressive marketing efforts of software companies such as Ariba, Oracle, CommerceOne, and SAP, executives of established companies were pushed into the new world of web-based data exchange. In 2000, there was a rapid introduction of these Internet exchanges in such vastly different industries as retailing, healthcare, automotive, staffing, and basic raw material commodities. The hype to join these "exchanges" was unbearable. Management was told that just by forming an exchange to pass data to customers and suppliers, all sorts of ills magically would be cured. Everyone was into business-to-business (B2B), regardless of whether they knew what it meant or how to use it. Life was going to be different and good, and if you didn't understand that, you were behind the new electronic eight ball.

Almost every industry in America was pushed to get into a B2B exchange before they were left behind in the dust of the new electronic age, as was threatened in Michael Lewis's book *The New New Thing.*[?] The race was on, and every self respecting CEO was asked to consider joining an industry-sharing exchange with competitors, an internal private exchange with their own suppliers, or both.

These electronic data-sharing tools popped up everywhere. The idea pressed by the fast-talking software makers and supported by analysts was to create marketplaces where business would be conducted online to increase speed and reduce costs. Somehow this was going to occur without the details being really defined. Clearly, the goals of communicating faster and streamlining old business practices were well intended. It was all happening, though, in a frantic and hurried atmosphere reminiscent of the Gold Rush days of the 1880s. Boards of directors were being asked to approve funding for joining something most of the members did not even know about, let alone understand how the benefits were supposed to be obtained. So companies jumped onboard for fear of being left behind.

The retailing industry created an electronic exchange without knowing what data to share. It turned out that sales data for retail goods is considered proprietary by many firms, and there was resistance to sharing individual sales by company among competitors. The healthcare industry started an exchange to share information on critical therapies to the general public. A number of companies offering similar healthcare treatments to individuals found that this was more of an advertising method than a true information tool.

The automobile manufacturers were not immune to this trend. The management of the Big Three was as concerned as any industry group that they would be considered too old school, or not "with it." They decided to create Covisint, a jointly owned exchange charged with becoming the industry's common data link between the automakers and their suppliers.

The ownership was particularly strange, in that the Big Three each owned equal shares. To make it look like it was more than a domestic industry tool, Nissan/Renault was pressured to come in, but only for a much smaller equity roll. Covisint was funded and managed by the Big Three, with their respective purchasing department executives as the initial board members and strategists.

Covisint is a great example of hype before substance. The idea never got off the ground because the premise was flawed from the beginning. Suppliers were naturally suspicious of using an exchange that their customers owned. The Big Three's managed exchange did not have a privacy policy or a position on which company owned the data that would be transmitted over it. But the pressure and hype to get the exchange up and running were intense. The Big Three used very coercive tactics to force suppliers to both join the exchange and to use it for data transmission. Even the Federal Trade Commission buckled under pressure for approval and waived its antitrust review with this encouraging statement by its chairman, Robert Pitofsky, on September 11, 2000:

> B2B electronic marketplaces offer great promise as means through which significant cost saving can be achieved, business processes can be more efficiently organized, and competition may be enhanced. B2Bs have a great potential to benefit both businesses and consumers through increased productivity and lower prices.[3]

So optimistic were those words that you might wonder which party actually wrote that release in September 2000. But the atmosphere surrounding the creation of this concept was even more supportive. The Automotive Consulting Group estimated that the exchange would produce more than $174 billion in savings by 2005, and the media reported that the Big Three were hoping the exchange could be taken public through an IPO with a value of more than $5 billion. It all seemed too good to be true—and it was.

As of this writing, Covisint has generally failed to achieve most, if not all, of its original goals. After a series of rotating CEOs, the Big Three installed one of its most vocal founders, the retired head

of GM purchasing, as Covisint's last major CEO. The supplier suspicion only increased upon his appointment, and many refused to
join in any substantive manner. Each of the Big Three insisted that
suppliers sign up and utilize the exchange, even though there was
little apparent value for their suppliers. This heavy-handed action,
coupled with their publicly stated intent to profit from the eventual
sale of the exchange as the Internet boom continued, created enormous mistrust. Plus, it was an extremely costly experiment. The Big
Three invested a reported total of more than $500 million to get
the exchange up and running, but it has yet to report a profit. After
a series of reduction and cost-cutting efforts, the exchange was sold
to Compuware in early 2004 for a fraction of the original investment. The Big Three were forced to take a write-off for the lost
value, and the idea seems to be dead—or, at least, severely reduced
in concept.

Covisint died an early death because it was a half-baked idea
that the general business public saw as a "get rich quick" scheme
by the Big Three to both tap into the hype of the Internet craze at
its height and to extract value from suppliers.

The auto companies are not alone in this experience. Many
other companies in industries such as healthcare and retailing have
been forced to write off or revalue their investments in web-based
exchanges. The general idea of web exchanges might have been a
little ahead of its time, and some are still functioning in reduced
capacities. They are all merely tools in a larger management kit to
facilitate firms to talk to each other and to exchange data quickly
and cheaply. The business world has reduced its expectations of the
instantaneous solution, once touted by these types of exchanges, as
the overall enthusiasm of the Internet has been reduced.

But Covisint failed also because it was ill conceived, created by
people who essentially still believe in adversarial commerce and

don't understand the nature or purpose of collaboration. Other exchanges have worked because they were more open and did not create the atmosphere of suspicion and mistrust that Covisint did. The fact that the Big Three did not consult with their suppliers on the value or idea of their internally owned, managed, and controlled exchange speaks volumes about why the supplier community resisted it so strongly. This was just another example of adversarial, one-sided commerce. It further showed that, when the Big Three companies are really imaginative and work together, they look for their own profits over that of their chain. Hopefully, now that the idea has been fairly well proven to be flawed, the Big Three will look to other ways to bring about real collaboration.

This example also shows that it will take more than hope to institute real change in old line industries. It illustrates that collaboration doesn't occur just because a tool is put into place—it has to be managed and led. Just forming an entity and hoping that it will bring about collaboration is missing the point of the concept. This is not some "Field of Dreams" that occurs without planning, effort, and a lot of coordination. Unfortunately, the failure of these rather poor attempts might have cast a negative image on real efforts underway to increase the working relationships between companies.

Where the idea of managed collaboration is really understood and practiced, real strategic advantage is gained. Other companies have been even more successful as they adapt and refine the way to streamline their relationships and free up the power of working closely with other companies.[4] This is much more than a theoretical concept; it is being increasingly put into practice today. The current economic system remains firmly entrenched in many industries because many executives still believe there is no other mechanism by which to operate. What those managers need is a successful example of collaboration. The Chrysler Extended Enterprise is one that we will examine next to show that the concept is more than a mere theory.

Endnotes

1. David N. Burt and Michael F. Doyle, *The American Keiretsu* (Homewood, IL: Business One Irwin, 1993).

2. Michael Lewis, *The New New Thing: A Silicon Valley Story* (New York: Penguin, 2001).

3. Robert Pitofsky, FTC Chariman. "FTC Terminates HSR Waiting Period for Covisint B2B Venture" FTC press release, September 11, 2000. http://www.ftc.gov/opa/2000/09/covisint.htm.

4. The Chrysler example is used repeatedly here because of its size, its scope, and the author's personal knowledge of how it functioned.

7

THE EXTENDED ENTERPRISE® CONCEPT

In his excellent book on collaboration, *Trusted Partners*,[1] Jordan Lewis outlines his extensive research showing how companies use and implement collaboration. One of his key points is that collaboration needs to be nurtured and managed; it doesn't happen naturally because our current system is so biased against it. Although collaboration is based on the most natural of human tendencies, the desire to feel associated with a larger group to accomplish a task, these efforts must be consciously put into practice. This is exactly what Chrysler Corporation's management did during the last decade. The example of the Chrysler Extended Enterprise and its success is one that has been used in numerous books, articles, and case studies over the past few years. It is a story that also is applicable to many other industrial situations beyond automobile manufacturing. Because it was successfully implemented in an industry that perfected adversarial commerce, it can serve as an example for other industries.

Automotive Commerce: The Good, the Bad, and the Really Ugly

The auto industry operates on size, volume, and leverage. Aside from a home, the single largest purchase most Americans make in their lifetime is their automobile. And they buy cars and trucks a lot more frequently than homes. The volumes of mass production are truly amazing. In a normal year, more than 15 million cars, SUVs, and light trucks are sold in the United States. Worldwide production exceeds 40 million. Multiply those numbers against the average selling price of $20,000, and it makes an economic force of $300 billion in the United States alone. Few other industries come close to that impact on the nation's economy.

The sheer size of the auto industry has influenced the management styles that are used to run it. Clearly, when you are the largest consumer of a given commodity, such as steel, you wield considerable influence. In the case of steel vs. autos, the two sides did try to work together but still failed. The auto industry and the U.S. steel industry grew up together, but when steel manufacturers from Canada and other countries entered the U.S. market, the auto industry was quick to jump on their bandwagon under the name of cost competitiveness. The market forces and our legal structure kept the auto and steel industries from working as close as they could have to solve their mutual problems. They let market forces and competition slowly force the large U.S. steel companies into reorganization. It was a wrenching process that took far too long to work through. We now have a much smaller domestic steel industry supporting a much smaller domestic car industry. Some economists say this was the appropriate use of leverage.

The issue is not the fact that leverage exists, but more in the way it is used. From its infancy, the automobile industry has been a mixture of power and personality. Wielding power can be intoxicating, and the people who manage the auto industry sometimes have let it impact their styles. One area in which that is most clear is in the purchasing departments of each of the Big Three.

Purchasing power in negotiation is always influenced by the size of the purchase or the buy. When companies are making commitments for enormous quantities, it is easy to see how that leverage turns into raw power. It even affects the way people behave. Early in my career at Ford, I remember a fellow trainee coining the expression "No boat, no quote!" This referred to the fact that a buyer, even a trainee, could order suppliers to entertain him or otherwise cater to his particular whims. In his case, he loved to go sailing and asked his suppliers to take him on their boats. He was not exaggerating when he stated that he wanted to buy commodities only from those sales representatives with large boats. Only they would get his quotes. Power and leverage go hand in hand, and sometimes the hand turns into a fist.

The "Game" and How It Is Played

The automotive procurement organizations are large bureaucratic activities that until recently were based on business transactions. Their job is to contain the commercial aspects of the relationships to their authority and to isolate the engineering, manufacturing, and marketing people from the "taint" of the commercial aspects

In theory, that works fine, but it also isolates, insulates, and builds protection systems into the companies.

The purchasing departments are aligned by the various systems and commodities in a car: electrical, body, power train, and raw materials. Typically, in any one of the Big Three automakers there might be more than 250 to 300 buyers working at one time, each responsible for managing a small aspect of the parts or services that go into the vehicle.

In addition to buyers, the purchasing areas are staffed with legions of financial analysts whose job is to monitor the suppliers' status. These analysts also have the assignment of pressuring suppliers for margin reductions by auditing their quotes and critically reviewing their overheads. This is all done under the friendly sounding term "open book pricing." When a buyer has a problem negotiating the initial price for placement, a team of financial analysts descends on the supplier like hawks on a rabbit. The result is much the same.

These procurement departments are still primarily driven by piece or unit price of the item they are buying. When you consider that a company might make three or four million vehicles, and each vehicle might use several of the same thing, such as 5 tires, 20 switches or hundreds of fasteners, it is easy to see why the difference of a penny per part quickly adds up into large sums. Therefore, negotiation and concentration is placed upon the per piece price of a part, to minimize production costs. This drives the whole organization into a transaction-based mindset that makes the current variable cost more important than longer-term issues such as warranty, engineering and development cost, and, sadly, often quality. This preoccupation with the short run is a major problem in all auto companies; it is further reinforced by the finance department's staff and the outside analysts who look at the quarterly profit as a primary guidepost of success and stability.

This short-run attitude often makes the companies and their procurement people miss the larger picture, and this trend downplays strategy in favor of cost control and cost containment. Each company's buying areas are measured on how much they spend and, more recently, upon how much they reduce the current cost instead of what they might be saving in the future for their respective companies. This sole focus on the current variable cost can have an immediate favorable effect on a firm's profit and loss statement. However, it ignores larger cost-reduction opportunities that are building in future costs, such as warranty, development, tooling, and capital equipment. These structural costs are often more important for a firm to control because they impact both current cash and the cost levels for products that are introduced in the future.

A horrible result of this current focus is the elaborate "game" that has developed with the suppliers. Because the business is decided and based upon current costs, new business often is awarded based on the lowest quoted cost. The supply base participants quickly figured out that a low quote was the major deciding factor and often bid at cost or even below cost to secure the business. They recovered their profits over time because the development process each of the U.S. companies used was so lengthy and convoluted that each part was changed several times, each time providing a chance for the supplier to increase its price for the design change. Suppliers often padded these design changes, but because the business was based on the initial quote, little was done to move to another supplier because switching cost time, caused disruption, and possibly produced quality issues. The suppliers figured out the rules of the game and adapted to it so significantly that they had little reason or motivation to bring new ideas or concepts to their clients. All they had to do was wait for the inevitable changes to come so they could increase their margins. It was as if the serfs in our feudal example had figured out how to trick the king into thinking they were subservient to him, while they made more money than he did off the wares they produced for him.

This whole scene resulted in both a frustrated procurement department that thought it wielded the power but that lost control because the auto company could not efficiently manage changes, and an equally frustrated supply base that looked for every possible change to increase margins to protect itself. The game was frustrating and difficult, but it was played successfully for years because the car companies could annually increase the price of the vehicles to the final consumer and recover some of the economics they had to pay out to the supply base. Like all good things, the game was played too long and ended when competition forced a change in the rules. This is even more true today. In an effort to stimulate the nervous economy immediately after 9/11, General Motors introduced significantly higher cash incentives to entice customers back to the showroom and to buy new cars. Their "Get America Rolling Again" campaign is credited with helping revive the total market and restore consumer confidence during that troubled time. The problem is that customer cash incentives are truly like drugs: easy to get hooked and very difficult to get off. Cash incentives have been a feature of the domestic auto industry for the past two decades. The "game" still hasn't changed.

Chrysler's New Idea of Coexistence

While the game of power and leverage was being played far too long, situations at Chrysler brought about a fundamental change to the auto industry's approach to business. It was based on the realization that companies exist on relationships with other companies much in the way people interact with other people. Instead of concentrating just on the short-term aspects, a longer-term view proved much more beneficial to both sides.

Departure—Iacocca Style

I arrived at Chrysler in September 1980, in the midst of the company's crisis that required the Federal Loan Guarantee Act to stay solvent. I left Ford at a difficult time because I had become disenchanted with the change in Ford's direction and because Lee Iaococca called and offered me a substantial increase in both pay and opportunity. I had been planning to move into the semiconductor industry after Ford, but I figured I could still make that move if Chrysler did not work out. After all, the move to Chrysler did not require changing locations, so my family did not have to move.

Chrysler sent a car and driver to the front door of Ford's North American Automotive Operations, and I was whisked off in full view of everyone in the building. Lee had made it clear that once I announced I was leaving Ford to go to a competitor, I would be asked to leave immediately. Making my exit in that massive two-tone Chrysler Fifth Avenue with a driver Lee had sent to wait for me was a touch that reflected on his style.

My parents never fully understood that move at the time because no one in our family had ever changed jobs. My father had worked for the same company for more than 40 years, and both my brothers were well entrenched in the banks they both worked for in the East. My parents were so rattled by my seemingly reckless move that they actually sent one of my brothers to Detroit to see if I needed counseling.

In September 1980, just before the Loan Guarantee was approved, the stage was set for a change in the whole industry. Chrysler was just launching the new K-Car, its hope for their future. Production of the new model was just beginning, and its older models were still bringing in revenue, although not enough to support the company. We were literally days from going bankrupt. In fact, we were technically bankrupt—what saved us were the suppliers who we convinced to continue to manufacture and ship parts for us to put into cars without being paid. We ran up staggering bills that we promised to pay when the government approved the loan. But until then, the suppliers were shipping on good faith and their belief that the company would not fail.

One supplier, Goodyear Tire and Rubber Company, continued to ship tires and built up an unpaid account of several hundred million dollars. Goodyear was one of Chrysler's oldest, largest, and most supportive suppliers. They were in a "damned if you do, damned if you don't" situation. If they stopped manufacturing and shipping, their revenue would instantly drop, creating their own set of negative financial problems. If they continued to ship, they were adding to an account receivable that was questionable, at best. The *Wall Street Journal* and other business press had a front-page article every day about our shaky financial picture, predicting that we would (and some said *should*) fail. But Goodyear and all the other major suppliers continued to ship. We actually printed the checks as if we had money, but, of course, we could not send them. Each morning, during that period of a couple of months, we met with our treasurer, who announced how much we could allocate that day in partial payment to keep the supply base supporting us. Many of the suppliers were in nearly as bad a shape as we were. Management had to work 24×7 to keep the company afloat and working. It was a scary and fascinating time.

Everyone in the company acknowledged that the reason Chrysler survived and eventually prospered was the supplier support during those dark days. The suppliers literally saved the day and the firm. It was a turning point in relationships in the industry. It opened the door to a new philosophy on how to manage suppliers, dealers, and employees. It also showed that every company in the supply chain was dependent upon each other and that this mutual co-dependence was a source of strength. And it helped to be in a crisis so that people were galvanized into action instead of sitting on the sidelines. To this day, people are still debating whether government assistance to industry is warranted, but Chrysler paid back the loan within seven years, with the company, its jobs, and its future intact.

During the decade of the 1980s, we reverted to operating like the other companies in the industry, with the exception of continuing the close communication and contact with our suppliers and dealers. Then in 1990, the same things almost happened again.

Because of the sudden drop in demand and the country heading into a recession, Chrysler's volume dropped to a point that its fixed costs were hardly being covered. We were unable to compete in cost, quality, or speed to market against increasing competition from the Japanese automakers. It looked to many that we were back in the financial soup again, only this time we could not and did not want to look to the government for help. Because that alternative was unavailable, we looked again to suppliers for help.

This time pressure for a rapid solution required soliciting the supply base for cost-reduction ideas. The suppliers accounted for more than 70 percent of the costs of a vehicle at Chrysler because of its heavily outsourced component level. The top 100 supplier companies were divided into five groups, and each group was assigned to one of our top five corporate officers to personally meet and ask for advice. In this way, the CEO and the president, as well as the CFO and the head of marketing, were dragged into the equation, even though they felt at the time that they were too far removed from the commercial aspects to help. Each officer held private lunches with the CEOs of our top 100 suppliers. Because of our size and leverage, these turned out to be some of the largest companies in the United States. The list included Motorola, Goodyear, ITT, U.S. Steel, and other well-known large firms.

The output of these informal lunches was amazing. Instead of offering piece price reductions, each company outlined how the cost of doing business in our adversarial economy was inflating our mutual costs. They complained that Chrysler itself was adding to the confusion and hurting its own profits by making the process of doing business with us so difficult and expensive. They showed how the Japanese were particularly easier and more streamlined in their business approach, without being any softer on competitive pricing. These executives independently confirmed that our commercial system, which was at that time similar to that of Ford and GM, was the place where major improvement needed to be made.

Birth of SCORE

As a result of what was revealed to us at those luncheon meetings, we formulated a plan to follow up on each cost-saving suggestion. The Big Three automakers had previously only paid lip service to these kinds of suggestions because it ran against their ego to believe that an outsider, a supplier, could actually understand their complicated system well enough to offer meaningful suggestions for improvement. It was a classic issue of self-centered control and ego. But this time, we felt that we had no choice other than to listen to the suppliers and to show that we were serious about improving our own situation as well as theirs.

It didn't hurt that at the same time Chrysler was struggling with its own cost problems, General Motors introduced the "Lopez Element" into the equation. We had the perfect foil to use to help institute our new idea of closer relationships. While Lopez was creating havoc in our common supply base, we decided to forge ahead by showing that we could listen to our suppliers and actually improve our mutual situations.

During this time, Chrysler formalized its collaborative approach under the label of the Supplier Cost Reduction Effort, or SCORE. This unique approach got widespread recognition in the business community for producing results in an atmosphere of cooperation. Other companies, including Motorola, John Deere, and many others, copied it. SCORE remains the single most successful program that improved both the cost structure and relation ships between companies. From 1991 to 1998, Chrysler lowered its costs by more than $5 billion solely through the SCORE program. More important, many suppliers improved their profit margins on the Chrysler business and devoted increased funding to technology that supported the new vehicle that returned Chrysler to profitability during this period.

In the past, suppliers had an understandable tendency to run and hide whenever one of their clients began talking about cost-reduction programs. But this time, instead of demanding another round of price rollbacks from our suppliers, we told them that we realized there were problems and inequities throughout our system.

The bombshell we dropped was asking them what we could do to improve it. After years of being browbeaten, whipped, and otherwise maligned by all of the Detroit automakers, it is easy to see why suppliers were a bit surprised by this change of attitude at Chrysler. Actually, they were shocked—there just wasn't any other word for their reaction. But once they became convinced that we were making a sincere effort to lower our joint costs, we began receiving some very positive feedback. And not long afterward, we began to see some bottom-line results.

The Success of SCORE

The SCORE program was in full operation at Chrysler from 1991 through 1998, when the company merged to form DaimlerChrysler. During those seven years, the collaboration program grew each year, providing ever-increasing benefits to the company. Because SCORE removed costs from our system, they were permanent, unlike one-time savings such as rebates or discounts that don't carry into the future. SCORE produced annual material savings in addition to our normal commercial negotiations. The result was that Chrysler's net material costs declined year after year. Additionally, the suggestions that came in from the suppliers compounded year after year because the parts often carried over for several years as the model remained in production. A third advantage was that these suggestions often involved the supplier absorbing development work so that Chrysler's own spending for technology was reduced. At the time of the merger, Chrysler had the lowest percentage of sales dedicated to research and development for new products, partially because we were leveraging the suppliers' own work. This also permitted Chrysler to reduce their time to market with new models.

The first ideas were processed in the new SCORE system during 1991, the year the program was formally introduced. Savings to the company that year yielded only $19 million. The data in Figure 7.1 comes from a speech to suppliers showing how the program's results grew to exceed $1 billion per year by that year and more than $1.2 billion in 1997. The cumulative effect through 1996 was more than $2.5 billion, showing how fast it spread and how well the supplier community received it. The total SCORE program saved Chrysler more than $5 billion in its material and operating costs through 1998. Detailed charts and additional documentation describing the SCORE program are contained in the Appendix.

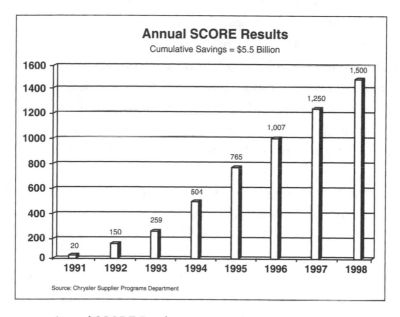

Figure 7.1—Annual SCORE Results

The program was based on encouraging suppliers to voluntarily submit suggestions that would reduce the cost of doing business with Chrysler. Unlike their competition at the time in Detroit, Chrysler did not demand that all the savings generated by supplier ideas be passed on to them. Suppliers were encouraged to keep some of the cost savings for themselves, to improve their own profit margins and to make the Chrysler business more profitable for themselves. In this way, the program became self-sustaining as word spread throughout the auto industry that Chrysler was indeed a better place to do business. Again, the adversarial nature of the competitors helped push suppliers into a closer relationship with Chrysler so they could share in the cost improvements. The unwritten but implied assumption was that the savings would be split 50/50, with half coming to Chrysler in terms of benefits and the other half being retained by the supplier. Some other companies (such as Ford) sent auditors into their supplier plants to determine the actual amount of savings to the tenth of a cent. Chrysler considered such auditing to be an unnecessary overhead expense and preferred to use the voluntary system to encourage additional ideas to keep the savings coming into the firm. The thought was that sending an auditor to verify a voluntary suggestion from an outside company might yield another penny or two, but it was so adversarial it would also ensure that the next idea would be a long time coming.

The SCORE program relied on internally tracking both the dollars saved and the number of suggestions submitted by a company. By 1997, we were processing more than 175 separate proposals per week, with a cumulative total of more than 9,500; we were approving fully two thirds of them. Figure 7.2 shows how the submission rates rose each year while the approvals leveled off at approximately 66 percent. This was an important dynamic to prove to ourselves that the program was sustainable. It also was useful to convince the finance people that the savings were not just from initial "low-hanging" fruit and would be permanent.

Initially, we were happy to receive anything that was above our normal negotiations over price. As the program caught on and participation spread, we were able to establish an annual objective of 3 percent of each supplier's revenue derived from its business with Chrysler to be returned in approved, real, and actionable cost-reduction ideas. When that level was achieved in 1996, it was raised to 5 percent, which remained in place for the balance of the program. The goal was simple: Each year, the supplier would return up to 5 percent of its total revenue from the Chrysler account in terms of approved cost-reduction items. We tracked the progress of each supplier and each of our own internal buyers as they worked together toward meeting these goals. Charts showing the relative rankings of the suppliers were prominently displayed in the purchasing areas in full view of all visitors so everyone could see the progress. Each month the supplier with the best idea, in either dollars or creativity, was highlighted in the *Chrysler Times* newsletter and on posters in the main lobby for all to see. This public recognition fueled the competitive instincts of the supplier salesmen, who never wanted to be topped by their own competition. We even mailed a quarterly report card to the CEO of each supplier to show him where his firm stood in relation to our cost, quality, and delivery objectives.

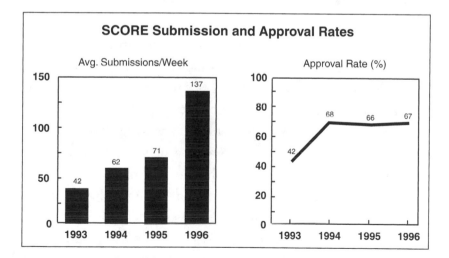

Figure 7.2—SCORE Submission and Approval Rates

The supplier community's overwhelming positive reaction to the SCORE program showed that communication was the most important element in achieving a cooperative and collaborative relationship. Some CEOs initially were upset to be getting such detailed performance data on their report card instead of having it go to a lower-level account manager, sales executive, or business unit leader. But Chrysler's experience from the Loan Guarantee days and those early top supplier luncheons showed us how important it was to get the senior leadership directly involved in the business relationship. This report card system is now in place at virtually every automaker and has become a standard practice across American business. The SCORE program did not invent the balanced scorecard approach, but it certainly helped expand its usage and acceptance.

Small Ideas Mean Big Bucks

It is true that most companies have suggestion programs that supposedly encourage the submission of ideas to reduce costs. What made SCORE so different and successful was that the ideas were tracked and our own internal Chrysler departments were held accountable to promptly process them. The suggestions were not tossed into some drawer to be forgotten or worked on at a later time, nor did they enter some dark hole in the company's structure. Each idea was logged into a simple system within 24 hours of being submitted to a buyer or engineer. They were assigned to the area of the company that had the most direct impact on its operation, such as engineering for product changes, manufacturing for process improvement, and purchasing for commercial dealings. Each week a report of open ideas was sent to the functional vice presidents, telling them of the backlog of ideas under their responsibility. A summary was also reviewed at the president's staff meeting so that the COO (at the time, Bob Lutz) could see the progress and provide his gentle push to his subordinates for faster approval action.

Lutz's personal leadership and support were a key to the success of the program.

The ideas came from all areas and in every shape and form. The objective was to get ideas in, quickly evaluate them for viability, and provide fast feedback to the suppliers on the disposition of their idea. In that way, we avoided the natural tendency to wait for the "really big idea" or to continually reprioritize the list waiting for larger items. Obviously, not all the ideas were good or practical. Many were old ones that the company had previously rejected. But each suggestion, new or old, required a new disposition from Chrysler to show the supplier exactly whether it would be considered or, if not, why it had been rejected. Rejections went to a separate higher review of management to ensure that the culture was not resisting the "not invented here" syndrome.

The program guidelines, shown in the Appendix, A.3.1-A.3.3, detailed the 21 different categories that could count toward meeting the cost goals. The ideas were things as small as replacing a cast aluminum engine part with a plastic one, for a 25¢ saving per truck. That idea yielded more than $150,000 annually: There were two on every truck, and we produced 300,000 light trucks per year. Or they were as large as one advertising agency taking over the media buy for all the dealers nationally, instead of having this done in regional offices. That concept reduced Chrysler's overall advertising expenditures by more than $7.8 million a year. No idea was too small or too odd to be rejected out of hand. The tracking and approval monitoring quickly exposed suppliers who were not cooperating fully, and they were pushed to participate, yet always on a voluntary basis. The competitive aspect of the program should not be overlooked. SCORE contributions also became the nature of future business awards from Chrysler. If a supplier did not have a good track record on approved cost reductions, new business was harder to obtain. The program was voluntary but had enough teeth in it to make it real and enforceable.

For the first time in years—actually, for the first time in Chrysler's history—we were actively exchanging ideas with our suppliers on how to make both our companies more productive. We discovered that, through teamwork, we could build better products at lower cost and create a more profitable future for each party. This was a situation that was uncommon to the automotive industry, as well as American industry in general. True teamwork between companies on a voluntary basis was rare, and continues to be that way.

The Extended Enterprise Philosophy

The SCORE program became a fundamental element of a larger program called the Extended Enterprise. This concept meant that we considered each member of our team an equal part of a value-added chain. This was a chain that didn't end at Chrysler's front door. Instead, it extended through us to the dealer and, eventually, to the retail customer. Instead of simply making a part and throwing it over the wall to the next level in the chain, as had been done in the past, this system got most of the suppliers to understand that they were part of a team working on behalf of the people who ultimately bought Chrysler's products. Every supplier, no matter what size or level, was an equal link in the chain.

The SCORE program became just one of several tools we incorporated into the Extended Enterprise idea. We boldly called it a supplier relations management philosophy, which became highlighted in almost every public appearance by our senior officials. We wanted the external environment of the press, the financial analysts, and the supply community to know that we were serious about the change in management style and that it was supported from the top. GM and Ford were forced to answer questions during financial briefings on what they thought of the concept. This helped differentiate Chrysler from other automakers in the minds of those groups that were very important to our overall success. The Extended Enterprise became accepted as a different way to work with our constituents.

In its early stages, the program was recognized in a *Business Week* survey (see Appendix, A.2) of relationships in the industry. With the Extended Enterprise in full swing, Chrysler scored higher in terms of having a true partnership with suppliers than any other American auto company. We scored higher than Honda and were just a bit behind Toyota. The program worked because of our willingness to let our partners be the experts. We finally admitted that they knew a lot more about their own business than we did.

We also realized that any supplier—for that matter, any one person—will be more productive and more efficient and will create higher-quality products if there is some sense of ownership in a project. The Extended Enterprise tried to pass as much ownership as it could to the supply base—all the way down to the lower tiers of the system.

In return, Chrysler expected the supplier to assume much more research and development work than in the past and to reinvest the profits made on the Chrysler business in new technology that would continually improve their products. This was the origin of an idea now commonly promoted by most large companies that the supplier should take the lead in supplying total systems, not just individual parts or components.

The Extended Enterprise is more than a concept or a theory. It was fully implemented and produced billions in cost and development savings for Chrysler during the 1990s. Although its name is still used at the successor company, DaimlerChrysler, it has been modified significantly there to revert to a more traditional adversarial style with which the company is more familiar. Unfortunately, it did not survive the infamous merger in any form other than name only. But the fact that this program produced documented results and improved the way that business was conducted while in active use at Chrysler provides a basis for continued expansion of its principles in general management.

The Extended Enterprise is based on the premise that it is important for a firm to directly plan and manage not only costs, but also relationships between companies. Treating companies as informed partners jointly working on projects, with assigned and measured targets, creates a working atmosphere that brings companies closer instead of keeping them separate.

Management become more engaged under this approach in the real business at hand than in the external aspects of PR or shareholder relations. This enables traditional mature companies in the United States to compete directly with foreign manufacturers that utilize a closer network to manage their suppliers.

This example has concentrated on the Chrysler Extended Enterprise, but it is applicable to much broader areas than supply chain management. The principles of closer communication, shared forward plans, codependence in profit margins, senior management involvement, and long-term commitments under targeted goals apply to any general management situation. Unfortunately, most companies not only ignore these areas, but they support the exact opposite: the protection of secrecy and compartmentalized planning. The effect is to stifle the cooperation between companies and to foster a negative noncollaborative atmosphere.

The Extended Enterprise worked because the management of a company, as a group, accepted the concept and worked to make it happen. This senior management cooperation was vital in establishing the appropriate supportive atmosphere within the company. The top operating officers from design, engineering, manufacturing, and procurement at Chrysler started functioning as an internal team. They were all housed together in a new building that was developed to stimulate team interaction. They appeared in Town Halls together and reinforced the message that the team was more important than the individual function.

It might sound academic, but this was a change in style that was completely opposite to the command and control bureaucracies that existed at the time—not just in automotive, but in many businesses. And they still exist today, ten years later.

This change in management became apparent not only to the employees, but also to the outside community. Some of it was natural, and some was intentionally highlighted. Chrysler highlighted the fact that its management team was a true team in every PR event or public appearance we could manage. For example, Francois Castaing, Tom Gale, and I (in our respective engineering, design, and supply functions) were the only company officers who attended one of the investor conferences held for the Wall Street analysts who cover the industry. The other companies showed up with their CFOs and investor relations spin doctors, but we wanted to highlight that the operations side of the company was linked together and that we understood larger business issues than those represented by our traditional job titles. The investors loved it because they heard directly from people running the company, not some filtered financial mouthpieces who were worried about putting the appropriate investor spin on information. The financial community recognized Chrysler for having the best investor relations in the industry because of this direct and open approach. This also helped greatly to be compared favorably to the relatively control-oriented management of our domestic competition.

The lesson learned is that implementation should not be left to chance. It has to be forced, cajoled, hyped, and pushed from the top. It also helped to provide a focus for the culture change that was required. This joint application of collaboration and the institutionalizing of team management produced tremendous results: It saved the company and made it the most profitable one in the industry in 1998—and a target for our subsequent acquisition by Daimler-Benz.

What happened to DaimlerChrysler afterward was played out in the press, the courts, and the market. It is obvious that the new management broke up the team concept that was so foreign to the European culture of Daimler-Benz. Although external market situations might be the reason for their current financial problems, the forced change in style back to a traditional way of managing has also been a major contributing factor. The difficulty of implementing the DaimlerChrysler merger is much more complicated than apparent to the outsider and should not be used to discount the success of the original Extended Enterprise.

The Extended Enterprise concept is much larger than a tool in supply chain management. It represents a completely different way to work, with outside partners in a collaborative fashion. It is based on building trust and establishing joint goals and measuring progress toward them. It is not a soft, philosophical approach, but it does utilize aspects of human behavior that we have often overlooked in our blunt use of power and leverage. It requires much more skillful planning and strategic thinking to implement, and that is why some companies consider it too dangerous to even contemplate using. But this reluctance is a reflection on the riskadverse, tradition-bound nature of our system of management. Instead of watching our remaining manufacturing and industrial base in the U.S. erode, it is time to try something other than the time-honored but flawed way we run our businesses.

Chrysler's successful implementation of the Extended Enterprise philosophy shows that collaboration can produce the same kind of short-term financial results that can be obtained under the traditional methods. The real advantage of using collaboration is the longer-term benefits from establishing meaningful and real relationships between companies beyond the short term. As seen at Chrysler, these benefits include reduced internal research and development, and more efficient allocation of internal resources. Critics of the collaboration method often miss the advantages of these longer-term benefits because they are too focused on the current financial picture. As the examples in the Appendix show, the Extended Enterprise and its SCORE program produced savings in both the short *and* the long term. The implementation experience can be applied in other situations by using a few standardized steps.

Endnotes

1. Jordan D. Lewis, *Trusted Partners—How Companies Build Mutual Trust and Win Together*, (New York: The Free Press, 1999).

8

COLLABORATION
DOESN'T MEAN "SOFT"

The advantages of collaborative relationships over the more common negative command and control types of business should be clear to you by this point. Working closer to the entire extended enterprise of a firm is not a new approach, yet it has not been as widely adopted as it should be. Executives continue to view this approach as very controversial, which is one reason it hasn't gained wide acceptance. Resistance to adopting collaboration is usually centered on the commonly held misconception that using collaborative techniques is somehow a softer and less demanding approach than traditional means. This chapter outlines why that is incorrect and shows how collaboration can work successfully, even in a very hostile environment.

As when any new idea is introduced, often the resistance to adopting a collaborative approach comes from the fear of the unknown. Some well-known and well-respected leaders initially rejected the Extended Enterprise® because it used trust as its primary element. Anyone brought up, educated, and trained under the command and control system rebelled at the thought of letting go of rigid authority and giving more responsibility to groups that were previously under control. That was just the reaction of Jack Welch to the Chrysler SCORE program.

General Electric is a major supplier of numerous components and materials to the automobile industry. It supplies everything from silicon glue to electrical components, to the plastic used in dash panels and structural parts, to vehicle financing and the factoring of receivables from other suppliers. GE is everywhere in the auto business, just as it is in almost every other industry. This is a great company, and Jack Welch became famous as the most respected business leader of the 1990s. That's why when his Detroit sales executive Al Febbo called one day and said Welch wanted to have a discussion about what Chrysler was up to in supplier relations, I quickly jumped at the opportunity.

Welch and I were attending the same event in Washington, D.C., and, although we were arriving by separate aircraft, his office arranged for us to share a ride to the event from Reagan National Airport into downtown. It was an amazing experience to ride in a limo while being peppered with questions about how SCORE worked and the idea of letting suppliers be responsible for their own costs. Welch listened and soaked in the basis of the concept, but he remained unconvinced that there were enough benefits to warrant changing from a system of strong direct control and pressure. But he was interested enough to send out his vice chairman, John Opie, to our new technology center to get a firsthand in-depth explanation.

Opie came to Detroit and spent the day with the Chrysler procurement and engineering teams. He saw how the internal teamwork within the company helped foster an atmosphere that permitted a collaborative approach with our outside suppliers that really works. Al Febbo said later that Opie went back and reported that Chrysler was doing something unique and that it seemed to be working. The only problem was that Jack Welch remained unconvinced that it could be applied universally. He felt that whatever was happening at Chrysler was so unique that it would not be easy to implement into another situation, such as GE, and felt that the more traditional approach was better for his company.

We were disappointed—not because he didn't like what we were doing, but because he felt that it was a "one-off" kind of program that worked only because of our strange and different circumstances. He was very gracious to us, but clearly he thought we were dangerously too close to being too soft with our suppliers, including GE. He felt that GE was making progress without needing to modify its whole approach to the way business was conducted. He might have been right for the GE situation, but he missed the point that collaboration might be useful and successful in some instances and might not be appropriate in others. Our disappointment was not only in his rejection of the approach for GE, but in not giving it some endorsement in other situations for companies with less leverage, influence, or profitability than GE has experienced for some time. He also missed the impact that the program had on establishing longer-lasting relationships that can help companies with fewer resources than GE become competitive in an aggressive marketplace.

Jack Welch's rejection was disappointing but had little effect on the success of the program within Chrysler. By using the coordinated elements of the Extended Enterprise, including the SCORE cost-improvement program, Chrysler was able to remove more than $5 billion from its material cost structure between 1991 and 1998, and was able to gain additional millions in access to advanced technology research and development through its suppliers. The program clearly was successful and worked. With a focused management team with a clear purpose, the situation at Chrysler obviously helped ensure the early success. But it was not a unique situation. The fact that the major premise of closer collaboration between companies had been copied from the Japanese automobile Kieretsu system, which is extremely successful and long-lived, shows that the idea is sustainable. The problem is less that the idea is novel and different than that our current commercial system is biased against efforts to change it.

Resistance from Traditional Roles

For years, the best business schools in the world have been in the United States. They have each been turning out classes of hundreds of MBAs who are trained in both the art of business and individual accomplishment. The case study system, which is widely used in graduate business schools, lends itself to individual analysis. The most popular area of concentration until recently in MBA programs has been in the financial area, stressing how to operate in an environment steeped in the command and control style we have previously described. Many of the CEOs who run our largest corporations graduated from those schools with training on how to operate in the current financially dominated systems. They are the people who are managing the large companies in this country, and they are the ones who provide some of the resistance to using collaborative business cultures. The use of transparent data, as discussed previously, is foreign to many current managers because controlling information is a foundation of their way of running a firm.

The concept of teamwork has been only recently introduced into the curriculums of those universities. Now we are exposing students to team-building concepts and projects that require joint efforts. Recent graduates from business schools are being prepared with skills to use in a different world than what actually exists in large corporations with embedded cultures. But the good old boys still run the system, so currently teamwork is often at odds with the way many firms are managed. To move forward, more businesses will have to overcome the resistance by those in traditional roles.

As employees become better educated in team dynamics and collective problem solving, managements have had to modify their old military-style authority structure. But many of our graduates fresh from MBA graduate programs find disappointment in learning that their first entry-level jobs are governed by the old rules.

It is easy to see how this same attitude of wanting to overcontrol a rigid procedure can be extended from how a firm manages its own employees to how it relates with its other outside partners. The command and control system can suppress good ideas and get in the way of possible teamwork by suppliers. Changing that structure requires management members to change their attitudes. This also explains why such change might be viewed as "softening" the old system.

Jack Welch's reaction to Chrysler's experience probably was not unpredictable. He is a product of the current system. Most financially trained executives hold deep-seated opinions that tough control measures are superior to the self-policing and advance goal setting that collaboration stresses. The government seems to follow that belief as well: The new audit requirements of the Sarbanes Oxley Bill, for instance, insist on tougher controls for publicly held firms. It seems that Congress, and possibly the general public, believes that to prevent the misdeeds that occurred in financial scandals such as those of Enron, WorldCom, and HealthSouth, outside Audit Committee Board members should have more direct involvement in overseeing a firm's financial reporting. This is a predictable reaction to a problem: More rigid and direct control is viewed as comforting and beneficial. As a result of these new requirements, every Audit Committee is struggling to avoid micromanaging companies and still meet the intent of the law. The new requirements are well intended, but many boards find that they fill up time with checklists and mundane reviews, while missing the larger picture of how the firm is really operating. Sometimes more control is not what is needed; more responsibility and accountability for actions is.

The trick in converting managers with similar beliefs is to offer a simple but effective measurement system that both tracks the value of the idea and identifies related internal costs that can be eliminated by adopting it. The total costs involved in the lifetime of a product or component are the system costs involved in using it. Tracking those costs instead of just the variable costs of the purchase price or hourly wages is important in measuring the value created by an idea.

System Cost Tracking

The Timken Company is a well-recognized world-class supplier of high-technology ball and roller bearings that are used in almost everything that has moving parts. The company has been a major supplier to the automobile industry since it was founded in 1899. Timken products are found in the engines of almost every automaker, and it is no surprise that Timken is an important supplier to Chrysler's engine plants. Every day, it ships thousands of bearing sets to plants to be installed into engines destined for cars and trucks.

In the early 1990s, those shipments of bearings were made in specially designed returnable containers that both protected the product during shipping and were reusable, to reduce shipping costs. At the Chrysler plants, the production line had to unpack the Timken pallet and reload the bearings into other separate containers to feed into the unique Chrysler automated assembly equipment. This repacking operation created double handling, which added to the labor costs and the potential for increased quality problems because of mishandling.

During the early days of the SCORE program, Timken suggested that it could redesign the containers used for shipment to fit directly into the Chrysler assembly process. This would reduce the redundant labor costs and would improve quality. To pay for the newly designed containers, Timken offered to amortize the cost into the piece price it charged Chrysler for each bearing. This would enable Chrysler to avoid spending the capital outlay at a time when financial constraints were significant.

The idea was a great one, and its logic was immediately apparent to almost everyone—everyone, that is except the purchasing controllers, who argued against raising the variable piece price. That was because they were solely measuring variable piece prices of the component, not the internal Chrysler overhead for manufacturing to repackage the parts, taking into account neither the savings to the system in inventory reductions nor the quality improvements. Manufacturing used a completely separate system for monitoring its own plant floor costs, and it did not assign costs to the part level. Although the idea was sound, the system threw up walls to prevent its incorporation.

The battle of the traditional-minded financial experts (or bean counters, to some) required the heads of the purchasing and manufacturing departments and the controller's office to resolve this ridiculous internal dispute. Fortunately, the issue was successfully concluded in favor of adopting the Timken proposal. It is, however, a real example of how the existing systems and traditional measures can inhibit the adoption of new ideas. In the end, Chrysler paid more money to Timken per part, but the internal savings from the streamlined packaging and shipments more than offset those costs. In this case, virtually all the savings came from inside Chrysler, but it was created by an outside suggestion that raised the price. It took several months to get the "system" to recognize the total picture of the idea. It wasn't that the traditionally trained people were thinking incorrectly; it was that they had to be shown that their old way needed to change, and they had to break out of the mini rut they had placed themselves in by not looking at the whole picture.

Tracking system costs is not easily done, and most companies do not have the accounting or financial mechanisms to do it automatically. That is because our U.S. accounting systems favor the short-term definitive costs over ones in the future, such as reductions in redundant labor or warranty savings from actions that cannot be traced back to routine actions. But other economies and markets, especially in Japanese industry, pay much more attention to these longer-run eventual costs. They realize that the costs of a company are more heavily influenced in the design stage of development than in the actual manufacturing stage. But if a firm does not track the total costs associated with creating a product, from design through manufacturing and into its life expectancy with the customer, it will be unable to reduce them.

The Toyota Difference

The example of the old Chrysler system's rigidity is not unique to that company or to the auto industry. Many companies have firmly entrenched traditionally designed accounting systems that ignore savings on a total basis. Modern and efficient companies must consider the impact of so-called hidden costs (system costs such as warranty, customer satisfaction and retention, and internal overheads) just as much as they follow variable costs. The preoccupation with variable costing might be one of U.S. industry's greatest errors.

Within the worst industry for adversarial commerce is a successful example of how a firm can use collaboration to achieve superior results. That example is Toyota. More than just a Japanese cultural anomaly, it is a mature company that continues to thrive and crush its competition through a carefully managed corporate philosophy of defining what is expected of itself and its suppliers. Toyota follows this process with consistency and fairness. The company is not "soft," but consistently receives the highest marks in trust and relationships. The final coup de grace in the traditional mindset is that Toyota is also the most profitable and successful automaker in the twenty-first century to date.

When you listen to executives in Detroit or Europe complain about Toyota's success, you hear excuses built around traditional thinking. It might be true that the currency situation is to Toyota's advantage, that the company has the advantage of new plants and employees in the United States and Europe, and that it has ties to suppliers that are difficult to copy legally in the United States. All that being true, Toyota also has the advantage of the best-managed collaborative relationship style in auto industry and perhaps all of commerce. It is based on a culture that is more holistic than merely Japanese.

The elements of Toyota's overall culture combine to make collaboration produce a system in which trust replaces suspicion. Contrasting Toyota to the U.S. Big Three, the following major differences show the way it conducts business across its own enterprise:

Toyota Collaboration Elements

Clear definition of roles and expectations

Dedication to long-term relationships

Strict performance measurement with feedback

Transparent measures

Process dedication

The famous Toyota Production System (TPS) has been copied across the world by manufacturers of many different products. TPS stresses smooth production flow, with waste elimination at every step of a detailed and formal process. Toyota's manufacturing system uses transparent measures of output, scrap, cost, and quality that are promptly shared with all involved parties inside and outside the firm.

TPS has been proven to work not just in Japan, but also across the globe. Examples of it have successfully launched in both the United States and Europe. More important, Toyota has educated its suppliers and associated companies, and insisted that they utilize its elements as well. These are the same suppliers that service the domestic Big Three and the European OEMs. Although the Western firms have tried to copy the TPS method, they have had only limited success in its implementation.

Discussions with suppliers who deal with both Toyota and the Western OEMs show that Toyota's consistent policy of sharing information, building relationships based on defining expected values and goals, and providing prompt feedback produces more cooperation and joint development. This honest and open communication policy is the heart of building trust within the enterprise. Toyota's actions are collaborative because the company works closely with suppliers on new product development, but they are not arbitrary or negative. They are based in fact, not rumor, and the company's overall business relationships are viewed as tough but fair.

This atmosphere of fairness makes the Toyota collaboration system function so well. The various constituents know what is expected of them and know that if they meet or exceed those goals, they will be rewarded with increased business—business that is based on products that meet consumer objectives, not the cost minimization so prevalent in the domestic OEM auto industry.

Other Attempts to Push Collaboration

Other major Japanese manufacturers use production systems similar to the one Toyota developed. Says Dr. John Henke, a professor of management at Oakland University who has done significant research in supplier relationship, "Pressure on suppliers to cut prices is universal, but there are vast differences in the way that pressure is applied." According to Henke, the Japanese transplants apply pressure without resorting to threats, with more consistency, and in a greater spirit of collaboration than domestic makers. Henke's research led him to conclude, "The (component) suppliers tell us that (variable) cost is more important for the Big Three than it is for foreign domestics."[1]

Similar surveys (performed by consulting firms including Cap Gemini and Ernst and Young, and academic research at Emory University[2] and Case Western Reserve[3]) confirm the success and strength of the Toyota/Japanese collaboration approach. That approach was used as part of the basis for Chrysler's Extended Enterprise philosophy. As pointed out earlier, we at Chrysler had to modify the TPS system and implement it first in the supplier relations area before we could use it in our own manufacturing. It began to catch on with the suppliers who were hoping that some of the domestic manufacturers could change.

In his book *The Toyota Way*,[4] Jeffrey Liker notes that the success of the Chrysler program worried Toyota in the late 1990s. As he described it, "Toyota was concerned by these (Chrysler) developments. Up to that point, no U.S. company had shown signs of getting it right and developing a culture that could compete with Toyota. But Chrysler was beginning to get it right."

This point was verified by another independent survey (see A.9.1–A.9.3) of suppliers taken in 1997 showing that Chrysler had surpassed all of its domestic competitors in critical relationship areas. Chrysler was second only to Toyota in helping reduce costs, improve quality, and undergo continuous improvement. The Extended Enterprise had clearly turned around the old, poor combative approach.

It was encouraging to see Liker's observation that Chrysler was not only getting Toyota's attention, but was actually getting the company worried. Unfortunately, the Extended Enterprise did not survive long into the DCX merger, and the company lost its unique advantage. It became easier for the DCX joint German/American management to revert to old-style adversarial methods. Because the rest of the United States and Europe were working under that approach, it was viewed as more traditional and conforming.

Nissan Recovers and Improves with Collaboration

While DaimlerChrysler was losing ground, one other manufacturer was breaking out of the pack. Nissan recovered from virtual bankruptcy through the organizational talents of Carlos Goshen, sent in from Renault to protect its investment. Goshen's recovery plan for Nissan was to maintain its collaborative Japanese approach while replacing the supply base. This might seem like a contradiction, but it is another example that collaboration itself isn't "soft" and can continue to be used while companies are in distress.

Nissan became the victim of poor product planning and unimaginative design. The company maintained a keiretsu group of suppliers who were closely related to Nissan but were not world class. Goshen realized both the danger of a weak supply system and the advantage of the close operation they had enjoyed during the Japanese management's tenures. He opened up Nissan sourcing to other world-class global component suppliers but kept the elements of collaboration highlighted earlier in the Toyota discussion. It is a tribute to his organization and managerial abilities that Goshen was able to accomplish this feat. Nissan now is on a roll. It has great new products and significantly improved profitability, and, at this writing, is the hottest, most successful car company around. It is a success story of both exceptional talent and the collaboration approach with a unique twist.

It shows that a company in deep financial and product trouble can make major changes in its enterprise while still holding on to the principles of collaboration. In this case, Nissan was able to replace its old closely held supply base with a new, more global one. The new suppliers realized the opportunity and pledged their cooperation because they saw that Nissan was serious about making changes for the long term rather than quick fixes. Although the act of changing suppliers might seem adversarial, the manner in which it is conducted is the determining factor. Nissan followed the rules of collaboration by outlining the responsibilities of its suppliers, communicating its intent, and following through in a consistent and predictable fashion. Certainly, the results cannot be considered "soft," even though the approach was collaborative.

This example shows that it is possible to change an old-style, deeply entrenched culture into a modern, efficient one by using collaboration to accomplish it. The losing U.S. domestic auto manufacturers continue to follow adversarial tactics, whereas Nissan has recovered using the collaborative approach. This demonstrates why we must change the way we manage and relate to each other.

The Critical Factor Is Management

Other successful companies, including Dell Computer, have developed their own styles of collaboration featuring strict performance targets. The issue is not that collaboration means soft tactics or results. It actually requires more planning, forethought, and monitoring than the adversarial system, which relies on reaction rather than foresight. No one practicing collaboration successfully goes about it with a laissez-faire attitude. A collaborative program can and should have aggressive goals defined for all participants. The difference is that the goals are mutually set and responsibilities are clearly defined. In adversarial commerce, the goals are left undefined or constantly change.

The popular misconception that collaboration is soft stems from the misunderstanding of how to manage it appropriately. After the necessary goals have been established, it is essential that the progress toward meeting those goals be measured in clear, understandable metrics. The proper use of metrics can drive the right behavior as the organization implements the changes in style.

Organizations respond just like individuals to defined tasks and the clear measurement of their progress in meeting them. The more open, the better. In sports, the entire team knows that the objective is to win a game or match. The scoring is not only visible to the referees and team members, but it also is shown on giant scoreboards across the stadiums. The same should be true for the tough objectives and measurement of accomplishments under collaboration.

To dismiss the use of collaboration because it appears on the surface to be too warm and fuzzy is to misunderstand the concept completely. As with any other management tool, it is only as soft as the management lets it become. With the appropriate commitment, collaboration can yield better results in the short and long term and can provide a way to tap into the greater resources of the extended enterprise that traditional short-sighted methods miss. Collaboration remains a superior way to reduce cost and provide value over adversarial tactics that are poisoning the commercial relationship in some of our most important but struggling economies.

Endnotes

1. Author, "Big 3 Lag in Supplier Relationships" *Ward's Auto World* 1 August 2002: http://waw.wardsauto.com/magazinearticle.asp.

2. Mudambi & Helper, "Close but Adversarial Model of Supplier Relations in US Auto Industry," *Strategic Mgmt. Journal* Vol. 19, pp 775–792, 1998.

3. Diana Drake, "The Dark Side of Interorganizational Relationships," Knowledge@Emory, Dec. 17, 2003.

4. Jeffrey Liker, *The Toyota Way* (New York: McGraw-Hill, 2004).

9

IMPLEMENTATION STEPS

The need for a substantive change in management attitude and style should be apparent by now. The real trick is implementing the collaborative approach into a working organization. In the same way that history and tradition inhibit change in our total economic system, the established culture of a company often works to block a change as basic as the switch to working more closely with suppliers and employees. It is much easier to have a great idea than to put that idea into practice. However, a few basic steps will pave the way to successful implementation.

This isn't magic or something that is so unusual that it requires the assistance of a team of consultants. Although the examples you will consider draw heavily from Chrysler experience, the fact remains that many companies, from Dell to Visteon, have been successful in moving toward more open and mutually dependent relationships. Such relationships have been implemented successfully in older, mature firms as well as in startups. The fact that the traditions in our economy often vote against moving toward a closer relationship between companies should not deter leading-edge companies from making the effort. But as will be discussed in Chapter 10, "The Conversion Experience," the company must have gone through an honest and real conversion or transformation process to attempt such a change. This is not something that can be used as a stop-gap measure to achieve some instant results. The decision must be made to embark on a new course and to stay that course even when objections and difficulties arise.

The implementation phase must be planned and well thought out. There will be a large amount of internal resistance to overcome, and communicating intent and benefits becomes one of the primary areas for senior management to focus attention. Without unyielding signals and reinforced messages from the top, the attempt to break the mold of the past will be difficult, if not impossible.

One of the biggest obstacles is fear of breaking from the past and being considered different from a peer group. Companies operate within defined competitive groups, and what is accepted practice in one might not be so in another. Industries seem to have developed unwritten yet definitive guidelines for various business practices within them. Breaking those guidelines requires more than a deliberate plan; it requires a lot of nerve from the executives running a firm. The tendency is to follow the herd instinct by doing what the majority does, to avoid the criticism that being different might bring. However, being different is required to be a leading company instead of a follower.

The basic plan for implementing a collaborative management approach is much the same, regardless of the type of industry; the size or the age of the firm matters little. One of the basic premises upon which this concept is built is that businesses are more similar than they are different from each other. The parochial attitude and the built-in culture of management create the impression that a company is unique from other firms. These can be torn down. Based on my observations made during 30 years of watching different companies, it seems clear that the situations companies fall into and responses they create are fairly common and repetitive. Accepting that premise is the key to making changes happen.

Getting Started

You have already considered the need for a management attitude conversion to occur if changes are to be instituted. It is absolutely essential that the entire senior management of the firm be committed and aligned to make a switch in the way the company approaches its various constituents.

Implementation of a collaborative management philosophy requires a consensual senior management attitude and a clear, plausible presentation of the intended benefits to the firm and to the individual employees and managers. These advantages must be fully understood, communicated, and accepted by the enterprise for the change to take hold. It is essential that the objectives be mapped out and that the internal planning be thought through before attempting any policy or procedural changes.

This is one place where Chrysler and Daimler-Benz never spent enough effort or thought. During the 1999 "merger," the plan was to produce synergies as soon as possible, to convince Wall Street of the viability of the combination. The companies had vastly different approaches to supplier management. Juergen Shrempp claimed, both publicly in the initial press rationale for the merger and repeatedly in private internal conversations, that he wanted Chrysler's more trusting approach to be the lead in the new company. But he never reasoned through or requested a way to accomplish this. Nor did he anticipate the degree of resistance it would create internally from the Daimler side. Likewise, the other co-CEO, Bob Eaton, never spent time working to ensure the success from the Chrysler side. Without senior leader support and appropriate planning, the conversion to the Chrysler system failed and the new company missed an opportunity to change.

Several important and definitive steps must be taken to ensure success:

1. Establish a formal program.

2. Develop the communication plan.

3. Build a measurement system.

4. Involve the whole enterprise.

5. Remove internal resistance.

6. Build an atmosphere of trust.

Each of these steps has to be individually addressed in a plan to change management's style and approach to dealing with partners. We will go through them in some detail to show how they apply universally to almost any similar situation.

Establish a Formal Program

To launch any corporate cultural change, it helps to tie it to a formal program that can be promoted and in which results can be measured. Obviously, having a leader just announce that he has undergone a significant emotional event or promote his sudden, self-induced mindset change isn't very believable or understandable by the lower levels in the firm. Too much baggage has been built up to immediately drop past practices for a new slogan or idea. After years of following a certain behavior, there will have to be a conscious effort to wrap the change in some tangible concrete plan. The plan has to be tied to physical events that the larger audience that is always watching can comprehend.

The best programs have been tied to short- and medium-term cost-reduction efforts. These programs produce both documentable results and provide financial proof of the merits of collaboration over the adversarial ways of the past. Usually the need for cost reduction is readily apparent in the organization for competitive reasons, but that recognition is carried in a macro level and not at the individual personal level. It is necessary to convert the entire organization by appealing to the personal motivation of every individual. This is why the leadership effort cannot be placed on autopilot while the CEO continues to work the business roundtable circuit or jets off to some foreign junket. Personal attention to the details is required.

It is important to recognize that a wholesale switch in attitude and style will certainly bring out the skeptics who openly question whether it is the right time to take on a change. The most common objection raised by those who are skeptical of adopting a closer and more open management culture is the belief that hard financial savings are not realized with collaboration alliances. To counteract those beliefs, the cultural change should be incorporated into an aggressive cost-reduction program discussed later in this chapter. Without strong and clearly defined quantifiable goals, the program will look like a cultural change bonding session from the 1960s.

Effective programs must combine the cultural change with focused, real financial results. The formal program should come complete with a title or slogan catch phrase. This simplistic yet effective tactic permits easier communication and fosters the understanding that a coordinated change is underway, that this is not just a temporary whim of management.

Our program at Chrysler was labeled SCORE, the acronym for Supplier Cost Reduction Effort. This was the specific cost improvement (more positive than the term *reduction*) that solicited cost, product, and system suggestions from suppliers and tracked their progress in implementation. SCORE became well known in both the automotive industry and the broader area of supply chain management as a unique approach to mutual benefit for all the members of a chain. As the program gained momentum, references to SCORE appeared in the financial, business, and popular press, and it quickly became a key element of the Chrysler turnaround.

SCORE was incorporated into the broader approach that we labeled the Extended Enterprise®. This term was used to define the philosophy that suppliers, dealers, and customers were linked in a business relationship that extended beyond the walls of Chrysler's physical plants or offices into thousands of other companies. The programs of SCORE and the Extended Enterprise became so identified with Chrysler's unique style that they were continued after the merger of DaimlerChrysler. Unfortunately, SCORE had become too identified with my own personal role and with the idea of collaboration. After my retirement, Daimler management made a conscious decision to revert to more adversarial tactics in use by GM and Ford. As a program, SCORE was dropped and replaced by a linear programming model to force down supplier costs. Management did, however, continue to use the label of the Extended Enterprise, to maintain some of the excellent public relations aspects that had been created.

The importance of building identifiable programs is evidenced in the number of similar programs adopted by a variety of companies. Visteon, a major automotive parts supplier, uses the term $AVE (for Suppliers and Visteon Excel), John Deere had JD CROP (John Deere Cost Reduction Opportunity Program), while Motorola incorporated it into their Six Sigma Program. Whatever the name, using a short, clearly definable program for the broader cost and cultural change programs helps to galvanize both internal and external factions around the efforts. These clear programs permit all areas of the company to understand and follow the progress; without a formal name, it becomes another dreaded cost-reduction effort.

Develop a Communication Plan

When the decision to become a more open and transparent corporation has been made, it has to be communicated to everyone involved. This requires different messages to the internal organization than those used for external groups such as suppliers or dealers. Internally, the need for change must be clearly spelled out, together with a firm commitment by senior management to stick with and to support the new approach. Employees will look for signs of doubt, inconsistency, or back-sliding in management's actions. The expression "walking the talk" is extremely valid here. Management must outline the rationale and then establish an atmosphere that encourages people to change their old habits. The internal message must be repeatedly reinforced over a period of time until it becomes institutionalized within the company. It requires overkill to make sure that the correct message is getting through to the constituents.

At Chrysler, we held pep rallies, contests, and a variety of celebration events to highlight our progress in both obtaining cost reductions and getting internal departments to work together. This took some adjustment for the management because it seemed that too many of these events were more sophomoric than necessary in a large, established corporation. Yet showcasing both the results and senior management's support quickly removed lingering suspicions or concerns that the program was temporary and ineffective. Nothing was left to causal interpretation. When the first major financial milestone of supplier cost savings was achieved, we held a rally in our engineering departments featuring the Stanley Cup Champion Detroit Red Wings hockey team members. The implied image of creating a winning team both on the ice and within Chrysler was not missed by even by the most cynical old-liners. Celebrations with celebrities, T-shirts with the program's logo on them, and posters in the lobby areas are ways of showing the action is real.

External communication is equally important in augmenting the internal plan. The message here is slightly different. Although this communication also stresses the open team environment, it should rely more on fact than on emotional tone. The outside world is much more inclined to be skeptical than the internal members, who are generally favorably dispossessed. Here, T-shirts and banners are not initially of any value to get the messages across. Actual examples, including the dollar savings or other quantifiable measures, should be called out in newsletters and press releases. This publicity helps increase the competition among suppliers or vendors and builds credibility. It is important for the external communications to be concise and fact based, to avoid the "PR hype" impression that often comes out of corporate press releases. For this reason, the external communications plan should be tied to the financial reporting of progress for cost reduction, to obtain the most visibility from the financial and business press. Chrysler included cost updates related to SCORE in its quarterly financial briefings with analysts. There was no need to take out ads proclaiming the program or change in the *Journal*. The popular press followed when the success of the collaboration cost reductions become established. The outside world responds to the credibility brought by financial analysts and press.

Build a Measurement and Tracking System

To convince skeptics that the implementation is actually working and producing results, a measurement and tracking system should be established when the programs are launched. These systems should be broadly based and should not just be financial in nature. As noted, financial results are the measures that outside analysts and industry peer groups most readily accept. That is because the traditional commercial system uses numbers (profits or savings) to (primarily) judge success. Therefore, any measurement system must start with clear financial targets and rules for tracking results.

The SCORE program initially did not publicize the intended results. Instead, it offered suppliers an open measurement system that would give credit for price reductions, R&D absorption, tooling and facility changes, and warranty reductions. The purpose was to count any real savings idea, regardless of where it showed up in the company. That helped launch the program, but soon after getting it launched, we established a percentage of supplier sales revenue that was to be redirected back in the form of savings ideas. The first target was a 3 percent annual net cost savings, which was achieved in the first year of the program. Eventually, as the competition in the industry accelerated and inflation dropped to zero, the target was raised to 5 percent annually. Whether continual reductions of that level can be achieved year after year is not completely clear. In 2003, the adversarial approach in the global auto industry

demanded such a level of reduction. Companies using the collaborative approach are obtaining those types of results and are
simultaneously improving their relationships. The use of firm,
measurable targets documents that fact in the program.

The new measurement system, one that can track costs wher-
ever they occur, conflicts with the routine accounting systems of
most industrial firms. This cannot be used as a reason to not track
the ideas and suggestions from outsiders; it just means that the
financial area of the firm must be involved and brought into the
program. If they are excluded, the financial types can become a
source of internal resistance.

The measurement system must include nonfinancial measures
as well. This is because you are trying to measure the degree of
change in the corporate culture in addition to pure financial results.
It is critical that measures of softer results, such as the number of
ideas submitted, the number of team suggestions, cost-avoidance
measures, supplier research and development commitments, and
other items related to nonprofit and loss be tracked. The long-term
success of a program goes far beyond the short-term effects that the
accountants reflect in the income statement. Sometimes intangible
benefits pay off greatly in relationship management and help monitor changes in management attitude.

The system used to monitor both costs and ideas must be simple and accessible to the entire organization; as discussed in
Chapter 5, "Information Is Power and Sharing Doesn't Come
Naturally," the results should not be controlled by one activity.
Instead, the system must be transparent and open so that everyone,
inside and out, can see the progress made. This transparency makes
many executives nervous, but it should be done to build the credibility of the changes.

Involve the Whole Enterprise

It is important that the implementation be adopted and promoted across the entire firm and into its extended enterprise of dealers, suppliers, franchise owners, and even shareholders. To be truly effective, the attitudinal change efforts must not be allowed to become identified with a single area, such as finance, engineering, or procurement. What you are promoting is a widespread whole-sale change in corporate attitude that reduces the waste and idea-killing atmosphere of an adversarial commercial structure. Accordingly, the effort must be corporate wide and personally pro-moted by the CEO or head of the operating division. It cannot be turned over to some staff activity to monitor and follow.

Successful implementations have made the routine internal reporting part of the CEO's staff meeting agendas and have included references to the program at all appropriate public rela-tions venues. This is a program that requires leadership from the top to build the support from the lower ranks. The goals used to define the program should be reflected in the management per-formance-reporting system, to ensure that the various service departments buy into the idea. Tying rewards to behavior has been proven to be successful even in an adversarial environment, and for that reason it should be used in any collaborative effort to measure and reinforce the message throughout the firm.

Beyond the internal workings of the company, the public pos-ture of the company must reach out to its broader constituents. The very nature of collaboration says that it should not be limited only to internal operations. To gain the advantage, leverage, and specialization that collaboration offers, it must be expanded to the external members. When Boeing replaced Phil Conduit as its CEO in late 2003 and reinstalled Dick Stonecipher, who had been previ-ously retired, one of his first public appearances was to openly approach the head of the machinist union to work together on the new 7E7 program. Stonecipher was trying to show the union that he was making an obvious break from Boeing's previously adversarial union relationship.

The broader the scope of the program and management efforts are, the more successful the implementation can be. Engaging all parties—or, at least, making the offer to become engaged—can build momentum. If the program becomes branded as a "supplier," "dealer," or "manufacturing" program, it will be self-limiting. If all parties involved in the enterprise can say that they had at least a chance to participate, it increases the speed of changing the perception of the company. Even if the direct or short-term contributions of a particular group seem to be remote, its incorporation is vital.

Involving the entire enterprise is a difficult task. Many executives do not naturally reach out to outside constituents. Doing so doesn't require a personality transplant for the CEO. What is required is an organized approach to have those representatives leading the various areas of the company speak with one voice. In doing so, the outside world can see the teamwork atmosphere developing within the company. This reinforces the belief that the attitude change is genuine and that the firm will consider ideas for cooperation. A company that defers new idea consideration to higher levels usually slows progress. Delegating the management team to work together helps spread the concept to the outside participants.

Stamp Out Internal Resistance

Implementation will drag unless senior management champions it. Teamwork needs to be coached by the CEO. Pockets of people will resist change because they don't understand it, don't agree with it, or are afraid of it. As illustrated in the previous chapter, this resistance is natural and predictable. Whether it was the old Chrysler engineers threatened by the American Motors development method after the Chrysler acquisition, or the MSX European managers who did not want to adjust to a changing market, resistance occurs. In these cases, senior management must carefully anticipate who will resist and make real attempts to communicate the need and reason for the changes. But time is very short, and it is important not to get bogged down in trying to change frozen minds. It is far better to react promptly than to be lulled into the false security that the resistors have been magically converted.

This is the most important lesson I learned the hard way. We could have made the merger of DaimlerChrysler faster and more creative if the Chrysler side had been more forceful in taking firm positions and demanding decisions be made in the new company. It is my firm belief that when Bob Eaton announced his impending retirement as CEO on the day the new company was formed, we should have moved more quickly to fill the vacuum that his lame duck status created. As it turned out, we lost a lot of influence when he did not use his veto power against Juergen Schrempp over some organizational issues.

The day before the formal announcement of the business combination between Daimler and Chrysler, Eaton decided that he had to also announce that he would leave within a short time frame. When it was pointed out that this could make him less effective, he replied that he could not keep it secret. Although one can appreciate his personal conviction, the resulting difficulties that it created for the new company were huge. Eaton failed to take supportive positions during the Management Board meetings that I attended that could have quickly resolved many internal disputes. He had the equivalent of a gun loaded with silver bullets, but he refused to fire it.

The fact that the former Chrysler side did not use all its available ammunition to force changes in the new company appears to be one of the major reasons that the former Daimler management gained eventual control. That clearly was not the way the merger was intended, but the failure to address the resistance to change in the planning stage resulted in a new company that eventually became more oriented toward Daimler than Chrysler.

Instead of waiting for the resistance to fester and build, management must act promptly in replacing individuals who either don't buy in or, worse, only give lip service to the effort. Removing these people might be hard in the short run, but it will result in faster implementation and convince the organization that the changes are permanent and real. The longer management waits and allows resistance to build, the harder it will be to make the changes later in the program. Stamping out resistance and the negative people who foster it early helps ensure faster implementation. It also helps rid the organization of people who make life difficult under normal conditions.

Building an Atmosphere of Trust

The final and most essential element of the culture change that ties the implementation together is to establish an atmosphere of genuine trust throughout the enterprise. Trust is not something that can be immediately directed or legislated. It obviously must be built through a series of related and consistent actions undertaken by the whole corporation. When the decision is made to break the mold of the existing behavior, it is up to the senior management to make sure that commitments are honored and promises are kept. The environment of trust will eventually be a product of actions over time, but it can be accelerated if the management team consciously reviews its progress.

An example from Detroit at the close of 2003 shows how management's lack of awareness of the perception of actions can backfire if not coordinated properly. General Motors had announced in a series of presentations that it was seeking closer relationships with its suppliers. The company was in the process of reducing and consolidating its supply base for valid economic reasons. As in most U.S. industrial firms, its previous policies had been to constantly increase the number of suppliers through the years. It is generally recognized that this practice actually increases costs because it fragments volume and increases communication problems. Now, as in many other companies, GM is reducing that complex network to concentrate on fewer suppliers. Part of its commitment is to offer longer-term relationships with those that remain in its reduced base.

However, GM either showed an amazing lack of perception awareness or telegraphed intentional signs of renewed adversarial behavior when it announced that it could arbitrarily break any contract with only a 30-day notice period. The industry press screamed that this was the one of the most blatant uses of leverage recently seen. Later, GM senior management was forced to clarify this statement by saying that it would be used very seldom—and only then as a last resort for quality problems. The management members probably would have created more trust if they had thought about using those qualifications when announcing the new policy. Actually, if they were really interesting in building trust, there probably wasn't a real need to make the formal announcement in the first place. Actions create perceptions, and trust is built only through a consistent application of principles. Any deviation creates suspicions, even if it is not intended to do so. In this case, GM only created more confusion over its intent with the inconsistent message it was sending.

In his book *Trusted Partners*,[1] Jordan Lewis defines mutual trust between companies as "a shared belief that you can depend on each other to achieve a common purpose." Those beliefs must be based on establishing some basic conditions, such as shared objectives, honesty, and commitment in relationships. Even if those conditions are met, the respective parties must earn trust by acting consistently and openly. Management must be constantly aware that the actions of a few managers behaving badly can negatively impact the program and destroy the trust of a whole organization. We saw an example of this in international relations. The scandals created by the few people directly involved in the Iraqi prison abuse by the U.S. forces clearly reduced any chance of earning the trust from the general population in Iraq there in 2004. Lost trust is hard to recover or rebuild.

These are general topics to help introduce a collaborative nature into an organization that has decided to change its behavior and culture. The key is that such a shift requires a lot of planning and constant monitoring—even policing—to make sure that the desired changes are taking root. Management cannot just assume that the collaboration effort will take hold without constant nurturing and reinforcement. Having a financial crisis might make the timing better for such a change, but it still ends up requiring a lot of management fortitude and leadership. That's why it has been so hard to accomplish.

When the implementation process has been planned and launched, it becomes easier. The early successes bring additional response from the various constituents as they see that the firm is sincere in changing its attitude toward cooperation. As the program builds momentum, it grows through the most effective method of communication: word of mouth. The unsolicited endorsement of other business leaders and the positive impression they make can help shift the cultural change into high gear. At this point, the changes can move from implementation of an idea into a practicing philosophy that identifies and distinguishes the firm from its more ordinary competitors.

Endnotes

1. Jordan D. Lewis, *Trusted Partners—How Companies Build Mutual Trust and Win Together*, (New York, The Free Press, 1999).

10

THE CONVERSION EXPERIENCE

The Extended Enterprise® example shows the value of taking a different approach to business relationships. Chrysler was able to craft a unique approach that set it apart and brought in outside ideas for adoption. Reaching out for collaboration can be compared to someone looking for help in any social situation. The pressures of conformity and acceptance create a heavy bias against companies trying something new. Even with this bias, the implementation of the change can occur relatively smoothly, as long as there is strong and effective leadership to make it happen.

The first step in breaking the mold of adversarial commerce is for a company to recognize that the old ways of managing relationships based on power and leverage are self-limiting and less effective than other methods. A break from the past and the introduction of a different management approach are required. This might seem obvious, but the fact remains the built-in bias and inertia of tradition often mask the understanding that the current processes are resulting in waste and suboptimal performance. The need for change might be felt within the company, but the catalyst for it must come from senior management. It will not come up from the lower levels or the rank and file because the "system" of adversarial behavior discourages creativity and challenge from within.

Every company is in a different situation that seems unique to itself. The situations can be different, but common elements help to manage the change and the conversion from adversarial to collaborative. This chapter uses examples pulled from some personal business experiences that illustrate how to set up a favorable atmosphere to embrace change. But before something can be changed, there must be the realization that something drastic must be undertaken instead of a tweak to the existing system.

Nothing Helps Like a Good Crisis

The awareness that things aren't working well under the current command and control adversarial approach comes via a series of disjointed events. Suppliers start complaining above their normal level of noise that a company is squeezing them for profits and performance. Employees exhibit signs of more stress and start using explanations such as "That's what the management wants" instead of giving understandable rationales for their requests. New product development falls behind, but no one takes responsibility; instead, the delay is blamed on outside parties. Finally, costs creep up without advance warning, and everybody runs for cover. All of these conditions are indications of a breakdown in the management system. The sad point is that management's response is often to redouble the amount of control, auditing, and demands placed upon the vendors and internal employees. A couple bad projects or products can turn a previously friendly management style into something like that of Attila the Hun.

Sometimes enlightened executives or CEOs can see the problem of increasing adversarial climate and press for a change themselves. But these cases are far too few. In most cases, an impending financial disaster is needed to bring about a revelation—the deeper, the better.

As pointed out in Chapter 1, "Breaking the Mold," Chrysler had a history of being on the edge of financial trouble about once every decade. The company wasn't alone in experiencing the wide swings of feast to famine as the business cycles evolve. One positive result of these near-death experiences can be a realization that more drastic change has to occur to fix the problem. In these cases, when the company's back is to the wall, real, substantial change can occur.

Recognize That the Playbook Is Outdated

To make the change to increased collaboration, the management team must recognize that traditional responses don't always work. The tried and true standard response to a financial crisis usually involves massive and drastic cuts in employees, capital spending, facilities, or a combination of all these. This is often referred to as "right sizing" in reference to a company getting its bloated cost structure in line with reduced revenue or profits. Although these are the universally accepted approaches to profit improvement, they are merely reactionary and do not involve changing the nature of the work the processes used inside the company. They just result in a smaller firm in which everyone works a lot harder doing what more people did previously. A smaller version of an adversarial system will still be as much, if not more, adversarial unless changes in process are made.

The normal reaction of internal departments within a firm is to protect their turf, which is their very existence in the corporation. Because this resistance may be so strong, the CEO or head of the operation must address the issue by personally following up with the respective managers to ensure that they buy into the change and actively promote it. One particular European aerospace components company with significant technology as its core asset had fought its way back from financial difficulty that had surrounded its industry after the 9/11 tragedy. Although its critics had predicted that it could never recover, the company became no. 2 in its specific industry. This company is an old-line manufacturer that operates around the world in a very competitive environment. As it fought to recover, it pressed suppliers in all the predictable ways that companies use. It asked for rebates, initiated "equity" programs in which suppliers would fund development, and shopped for cheaper prices off-shore. In addition, it used its situation to reduce its suppliers by more than 20 percent in number. All of this was done aggressively and with some adversarial tones. Now it had to decide what to do as it entered a new program that required enormous development costs to engineer its next product.

In short, the company had to decide whether to fall back to its old style of relationship management, using the strong-arm tactics of command and control, or move to a more collaborative nature. The company's experiences in turning itself around made the managers realize that they needed the assistance of their suppliers in both technology and funding. They could decide to take the safe way and follow tradition, or they could try to use the collaborative approach, to set themselves apart from their competition and adopt a different style. They faced the fact that they would need to change their management style, their organizational structure, and some of their accounting methods. Most important, they would have to implement these changes internally before anyone outside would believe they were serious. They could not just stand up in front of their suppliers and announce that they had seen the light and were converted. That might work for some evangelists seen on late-night cable television, but not for the more cynical business audience.

Stretching Minds or Removing People

A basic problem for many companies seeking to change is the human tendency to reward the status quo. The tradition built into the system requires management to replace, remove, or "change out" some formerly good performers to make change happen. People might have performed admirably in the past, but that was under an old command and control system. Because their knowledge set and experience factors are based on the very system that needs to change, many of these people cannot react to the new approach being outlined. They need to be replaced or removed from their leadership positions, to avoid having them block the changes necessary. Their blocking actions would not be malicious or intentional, but merely a result of not seeing the reason for the changes.

Fortunately, in many cases, the new operating structure of openness, transparency, and frank cooperation encourages other people to come out of their previous shells of protection and readily embrace the new way. This action is "stretching" the management-development system. In almost every case at Chrysler, when we reached down into the upper-middle ranks for promotions to place people in assignments outside their traditional backgrounds, we found that they approached it with renewed enthusiasm and interest. Some cynics explained this as a way of people just sucking up to the senior leaders by telling them what they wanted to hear, but, in reality, it freed these excellent managers from the tyranny of the old system. They had seen the redundant checks and balance, the overcontrol and wasted time and effort to force conformance to the adversarial way. These "stretch" managers turned out to be some of the most competent of the whole organization and greatly contributed to implementing change at Chrysler.

One great example of stretching was Sam Messisa, a midlevel financial manager who was placed in the position of handling investor relations. This position was extremely important in explaining the company's message and vision to the institutional investors who owned more than 70 percent of the stock. Sam approached this new job with interest, humor, and understanding of the investors' questions, and his answers were a key communication element in renewing Chrysler. Instead of using stuffy PowerPoint presentations developed solely by the isolated finance staff, he opened up the presentations to include real, live operating managers from manufacturing, engineering, and supply. The investors loved seeing the real operations people from the company, and Sam's open approach greatly contributed to getting the word out about how and why we were different from GM and Ford, and the ways we were reducing costs.

Sam approached his job with enthusiasm and directness. He answered questions from analysts promptly and clearly, without the usual "corporate babble" often used to skate around difficult issues or topics. He also did this with a staff of two: a secretary and one analyst. This group performed so well that the analysts who covered us recognized Chrysler as having the best investor relations in our industry. This was primarily because the person in the job tried out new ideas and was not stuck in the tradition of the past.

Listen to What Really Is Happening

These examples also point out that senior management needs to become totally involved and personally committed to making a change to collaboration. Above all, they need to listen closely to what their employees, vendors, and dealers are telling them about the way their company operates. Years of conditioning have led these groups to tell management only what they want to hear. That is the way they preserve their jobs and their place in the corporate hierarchy.

Listening objectively, having removed suppliers' fear of reprisal, helped the Chrysler executives see that the common follow-the-lead-dog theory of management was not working in their case. The auto industry had become too conforming and too alike in its management practices and style. The luncheon discussions we had with our top suppliers showed us that we were not as smart as we thought we were. The employees and suppliers were pointing out examples in which Chrysler was actually adding costs instead of reducing them.

Another example of how to listen came from Motorola. In an executive luncheon, the CEO asked us if we were really serious. He said that the Chrysler specification for waterproofing grease in our automotive electronic engine controller was the same spec as used on the Space Shuttle cargo bay doors. This expensive and hard-to-obtain grease added $4 to every car and could be substituted with common silicon grease. They had proposed this change to Chrysler before but, at that time, were told to continue blindly following the spec. This time, we listened.

Once again, the onion was peeled back and the true story was revealed to Chrysler management. The command and control business system was adding costs without any incremented customer benefit. What appeared to be common-sense proposals had been rejected by a system that did not encourage independent thought or suggestions. The problem was not with the employees on either side; it was with the way business was conducted. Because we were in a real financial crisis, we decided to make a dramatic turn and open ourselves up to a more collaborative and supportive environment to save the company. The senior management members were convinced and were working as a team to institute change, but the hard part to come was implementation in a company of more than 100,000 employees. That became the exciting part.

The Motorola example convinced the Chrysler management that there was a better way to leverage the supply base for new ideas and to help the company look at the cost/benefit relationship from the customer's standpoint. In this case, as long as the electrical connector was protected from water, the incremental advantage of using high-technology space shuttle grease was a waste of money. This extra cost could be eliminated to increase the profits or put money into another area of the car where the benefits were more noticeable to the person who actually bought it. But the engineers who specified the NASA grease were not bad people intentionally increasing the costs; they were just too closed in their thinking and were overkilling the specification so that they could be sure of the result.

It took some time for Chrysler management to realize that its own engineers might not always be correct or the most practical. The same situation is true in most companies that have a long tradition of success and internal pride. That is why the conversion process takes a while to spread through an organization and why it needs to be led rather than assumed. Not everyone will share the sudden realization that outside firms or lower-level employees can have a better perspective on the work that is required. That is why having a crisis or a galvanizing event is often necessary to get the culture to see the light.

It took much longer and was more difficult to get the conversion into place at MSX International. When I joined the company in 2000, it had a long history of being extremely competent at performing outsourced contract engineering for major industrial companies. MSX actually turned down new customers and had more work than it could handle until the competitive pressures of the automobile industry suddenly reduced the need for its type of work in mid-2001. When we realized that the workload was dropping, I started to pressure the engineering management to reduce overheads and to look for alternative customers in other industries. Management's reaction to my request was to resist, claiming that all that was necessary was to wait out the downturn, and things would be fine again. It was the classic "hunker down" mentality seen in many other companies. It is actually easier for them to cut back, shrink, and wait for good times to return than to change the fundamental way they did business. The problem with shrinking and waiting is that no one knows how long the situation will last, and no one can predict with certainty that if and when it returns, it would come back in the same fashion. This is exactly what I was afraid of happening and what did actually occur.

In our case, the major automotive makers had also been using new analytical tools and software programs to reduce the time needed to engineer new products. Their requirement for outside companies performing the work we had historically performed was being eliminated by their productivity improvements. We were experiencing a shift in the way business was being conducted, and our engineering managers were either unable or unwilling to accept that fact. In the end, it took the combination of continued losses and eventual management changes internally to implement the streamlining we needed.

In the MSX example, the conversion never really took hold until we changed the managers in charge. The resistance and fear to accept the changes required were beyond the vision of the previous managers. The conversion process took too long and wasted too much time. MSX is not alone in this example. Many companies ride the curve of declining profits while watching their business change. In these cases, it also takes the pressure of a financial setback or crisis to finally get the point across.

There are countless similar examples of companies that wait too long before they attempt to break out of the mold of tradition—some never do. The point is that, to successfully change to a new culture, especially one that involves looking outside for input and giving up some previous control, the management must first recognize the real need to change. They must be convinced that the conversion must take place. Adopting a collaborative approach to management requires a firm belief that a break from the past is mandatory; it requires a cultural change throughout the entire company.

Fighting the Financial System

Converting the mindset of managers who think traditionally also requires challenging the way they count. In most large industrial firms, the financial and accounting systems have been in place so long that they have become institutions in themselves. Forgetting the references about green eyeshade accountants or the snide remarks from operating people about their controller's ability to count beans, the truth is that the financial system in any company has a lot of clout. The power and influence of the accountant has increased with the requirements under the Sarbanes/Oxley Bill and new regulations required by various oversight boards such as the New York Stock Exchange and the Securities Exchange Commission. The corporate auditor now has a direct line to the board of directors in any public company, and that elevation has further enhanced the power of the financial system.

The problem that traditional finance systems bring to the conversion process is that they are often based on capturing costs within a single activity. In Chrysler, we had a detailed system to track variable costs at the part level. Manufacturing rolled up its costs at the vehicle level instead of allocating them to the parts that were purchased. The warranty systems tracked total expense at the dealer level. There was no uniform or consistent accounting system to make the piece cost, manufacturing cost, and warranty cost all come together except at a macro level.

What was required was not a new system to replace the old, but merely an overlay to the ones that were in place. The same thing still occurs in many companies where the manufacturing, engineering, and purchasing people all have separate cost savings targets. This separation discourages ideas that cross functions because the total savings are hard to track. Without senior management attention, the internal system might reject an idea as too hard to implement. Even in this example, some controllers in manufacturing never got the logic. For the conversion of collaboration to occur, the measurement system must be loosened up to permit the application of logic. That is often harder to do than to say. Later you will see how to address this issue. For now, it is necessary to understand that the financial measurement system in most industrial companies would rather fight than switch, and this will be an obstacle to conversion.

Corporate Cooperation and Involvement

Big companies are like people with multiple personality disorders. There really isn't just one corporate culture; there are many. Each area or group has a unique history and story that makes each act slightly differently than the rest of the organization. That is because people need to identify with a smaller unit as well as with the entire company. Good leaders of internal departments try to build on that fact of organizational behavior and encourage the development of subunit cultures to motivate and gain employee involvement. This fact might inhibit change unless it is recognized and dealt with before any announcement of a major move to working more closely with employees or outside partners.

It doesn't help if only one area sees the light and tries to bring about a change as large scale as moving to collaboration. Just as the controller's office has to modify its approach to counting costs and savings, the rest of the company must join in the conversion process. The good intentions of one area can't make a dent into the corporate culture; there are just too many other groups internally whose continued influence is based on maintaining the traditional mindset.

Resistance will be everywhere, and it is natural. The human resources group will object to any unorthodox movement of people out of grade or level. HR's idea of stretching is making someone wait longer in his established career path instead of trying someone in a completely new function or job. The legal area will complain that it is exempt from any organizational change and provide all sorts of reasons why it is really different and needs to be left alone from change. Actually, all the staff groups will say that their jobs and charters are to be the anchor for the company to hold it steady. In actuality, they are usually correct. They are the anchors, but only from holding back the undertaking of a new course.

To be successful, the conversion effort has to be broad based and universal. It cannot be given the label of another program of the month, or of a program confined within one area to make its budget. It must be complete and must cut across the whole company. That is why implementation during a corporate crisis is actually easier than during favorable times. During periods of adversity, the logic that the old way is better falls away and changes can be more easily adopted. The problem is that when good times return, the tendency is to revert back to the old ways. That is why in the example of the European aerospace company, management would be under internal pressure to revert to the command and control style that existed before they got into trouble.

The answer to this set of problems is that senior management must become involved and engaged in the change efforts. If a company really wants to change its style, the top of the house must embrace the change and show visible signs that it is serious about it.

Seeing the Light Requires Removing the Shades

When the senior group agrees collectively to undertake a change process, the reason for it and the advantages that it will bring must be communicated to the entire company. Clearly, that doesn't mean that the CEO must call an all-hands meting and announce, "We have seen the light." It means working to point out the inefficiencies with the current system. The temptation is to move faster than the group wants to go. This is what happened at MSX International.

MSX is a company that originated by performing engineering programs for the domestic Big Three manufacturers. Although it is global, that was merely the result of its traditional customers being located around the world. In fact, by 2000, the previously separate customers of Jaguar, Volvo, and Aston Martin were brought inside the fold of Ford, the company's largest client. Fully 80 percent of MSX business in 2000 was with the three U.S. automakers (if you still include Chrysler as domestic).

Early into my tenure there, I realized that our customer base was both an asset and a problem. It provided a comfortable base, but one that was potentially declining in market share. The Big Three were again in a fight for their lives. We at MSX had a strategy that we would expand the engineering and business services we had so successfully performed for the domestic automobile makers first to the transplant and foreign makers and then to related industries, such as heavy trucks, agricultural equipment, and appliances. We outlined this to the senior staff, which embraced it with varying enthusiasm. Instead of working to make sure they really believed in the rationale, we were impatient to start implementation; the market was beginning to drop for our traditional customers.

We went ahead and held a meeting at our European engineering center in England to explain that we would be moving our direction toward new customers while retaining the old ones. Personally, because I had spent so much time watching the industry attempt to change at Ford, Chrysler, and then DaimlerChrysler, I thought this approach was self-evident. It was, but apparently not to my managers. We outlined the plan to them, and they accepted it with polite English manners, but they clearly were not convinced. They did not see that Ford and all its U.K. subsidiaries were about to undergo major cutbacks and felt that moving away from our historic U.K. customers would be a sign of deserting them. They were comfortable to wait out the bad times with Ford. The meeting was held, but the reason for change was not communicated clearly enough.

As a result, two years later, after major losses in the United Kingdom, we had to consolidate our U.K. headquarters and terminate more than 50 percent of the head count. We were unsuccessful in getting management to see the light, and we had to cut back to restore profitability for future growth. It was a tough lesson to learn, having come from the Chrysler experience where this worked so well and was relatively easy to get the message across. In the MSX experience, it was much more difficult because the management was not all on the same page. This was a lesson learned the hard way that the conversion experience isn't easy, even having lived through one.

These lessons boil down to a simple fact: The need for change is usually not apparent to most organizations. To make a change to the collaborative approach, senior management must be personally and firmly convinced that they can succeed by working more closely with both employees and suppliers. That conversion process must be led, not assumed, and must be managed as it is rolled out.

A Dedicated Team

In the Chrysler experience, we were fortunate to have a team of highly skilled, intelligent, and dedicated managers in procurement and supply who made the conversion process much easier. Two people really stand out in vastly different ways, but each was extremely helpful in getting the entire company to see the advantages of collaboration. One was Barry Price, the director of production purchasing, who handled most of the annual buy, which exceeded $30 billion. In the early stages of SCORE's strategy development, he saw that getting ideas from the suppliers was the answer to breaking the mold of the existing "not invented here" mentality in Chrysler engineering. He was one of the founders of the initial SCORE concept and name.

Price launched the idea internally but did not grasp the full potential of managed collaboration. He believed that the suppliers should not be actively managed. The real hero in bringing the conversion at Chrysler into being was Jonathan Maples, who succeeded Price as vice president of supply. Maples now is a senior executive at Visteon, where he helped set up the company's integrated supply program and launched a refined version of SCORE that helped reduce costs by more than 7 percent in its first year. While at Chrysler, Maples saw that setting targets, measuring the accomplishment of goals, and communicating clearly were the keys to getting the results that could convince the rest of the company to make the conversion. His recognition that collaboration needed to be led rather than just left to happen brought the program to its highest point of success. He fought the tough battles with the controller's office over the measurement of system costs. Through his efforts, the entire company finally began to see that costs were buried throughout the organization, not just at the outside piece cost level.

The dedication of these two people helped move the company through its conversion process. They reported to me directly and were able to move the concept into reality. A strong and dedicated group helped keep the program in focus and pushing for success. Any conversion needs to have some key and well-respected leaders like these to help adapt the idea and bring new innovation to the concept. Every company requires a tailored approach to conversion and implementation.

11

BREAKING THE MOLD: MOVING TO COLLABORATION

We have seen how companies can become mired under the harsh ways of adversarial commerce. Whether it is intentional or just the result of cultural conditions, its practice can increase costs, reduce access to new ideas, and generally place all parties in an atmosphere of protective tension. The alternative is to use collaborative management tools to increase cooperation between firms. Although this approach is more difficult to implement, it can provide a new path for managers to revitalize their companies. But why take the risk and embark on such a new tactic? The answer is that the built-in tendency of companies to revert to the old command and control style of management is directly impacting our nation's economic recovery and progress. If something isn't done to change the way businesses relate to each other and to their own employees, the competitiveness of American business will continue to suffer.

Instead of working more closely together, many companies are wrapping themselves in a protective cocoon of isolation. This creates a negative tone that comes from a desire of corporate management to be in complete control and to always seek a dominant position using overt and aggressive tactics instead of more detailed planning or strategy. This leads to more friction in the everyday dealings between companies and builds walls of protection. If we don't reverse this trend, our industrial sector will continue to lose jobs and our manufacturing base will continue to erode as other companies from other countries that have put aside adversarial commerce succeed where U.S. companies sputter and fail. It is time to embrace a more collaborative style of managing relationships between companies.

Why Bother to Change?

Our present commercial system has worked better than any other during the past 200-plus years of business evolution in the United States. In spite of its many shortcomings, many managers are still skeptical of the need for making what appears to be a drastic change to our time-honored business practices. The truth is that we are running out of time, and gradual tweaks or adjustments just won't bring about the degree of change that is required to break out of our old mold.

The aggressive nature and strong momentum of foreign competition, especially from emerging powerhouses in Asia, represent a real and present threat to old-style practices used by American management. Companies in that region cannot expand by relying solely on their domestic markets. They have been looking and will continue to look at the enormous American market to fuel quick growth of revenue and profits.

The world's separate economies have become more intertwined than ever in history. Until recently, most American businessmen looked at China as a vast unknown market with little direct impact on them. Even though China has more than a fifth of the world's population, its relationship to us seemed remote. The same opinion was held about India, which many CEOs think might someday be able to break out of its poverty, but not during their tenure. These were considered places to use because of their low labor costs, but not to be feared as direct competitors because they lacked technology and knowledge of our markets. It seemed that they posed no immediate threat to our own market, and we could tap into their low labor base at will.

Yet, in just the past few years, China has become the fastest-growing market in the world for automobiles, construction projects, and manufacturing. The country has its own space program, and it graduates more technically degreed professionals than any other country in the world. China is also one of the largest buyers of U.S. government bonds, and by pegging their undervalued currency to our dollar, the Chinese have tied themselves to our own fiscal policies. Today a severe drop in the Chinese economy would have a direct effect on the U.S. economy, which was not the case a few years ago. Meanwhile, India has become the center for software development, the tool that drives the expansion of information technology around the world. The engineering skills of its citizens now rival those of the United States and other western nations, but at a fraction of our cost levels. Together these two Asian powerhouses represent 40 percent of the world's working-age population and only 18 percent of the purchasing power.[1] U.S.

manufacturers are falling over themselves as they scramble to place business in those areas even though they might not have a clear idea of how to enter, utilize, or capitalize on the advantages. The old ways of trying to make foreign subsidiaries and ventures look like miniature clones of U.S. companies have been eclipsed by the rapid rise of local Asian companies. Who would have predicted that domestic Chinese-manufactured automobiles would someday show up in the United States to compete with the mighty Big Three? Probably not the same managers who thought that Honda would never sell anything here larger than a motorcycle. And this is not limited just to automobiles. The Chinese company Haier has become one of the largest sellers of refrigerators in the United States by exporting not from China, but from a plant in South Carolina, where they make up to 200,000 units a year. Times have indeed changed, but our management practices are still based on the old ways of using power and leverage.

Bad Behavior at U.S. Automakers

Adversarial commerce is the most widespread and blatant in the American automobile industry. It is the largest industry on Earth in terms of revenue, employment costs, and scope of related industries. Severe challenges face every auto manufacturer, with the U.S. companies having been under threat for the past 30 years. The domestic Big Three (including the U.S. side of DaimlerChrysler) are in a life-and-death struggle for market share and consumer demand. For decades, they have been in a desperate battle for survival against more nimble foreign competition. Unfortunately, they continue to lose share and product innovation to foreign manufacturers. Their management has followed the traditionally accepted approach to reduce costs by shedding jobs and industrial capacity. They are using old-style tactics to fight a different kind of war, just as the British did against the U.S. colonists. Each of the domestic automakers remains in a fight for its economic life, and the outcome is neither clear nor certain. The problem is, they are losing most of the battles—and perhaps the war itself.

Faced with possible economic extinction, the automakers are fighting back with increasingly arbitrary tactics, just as animals fight when mortally wounded. Because they operate in an open industry—one in which the suppliers and supporting firms deal with both the domestic and foreign car makers—the continued use of adversarial commerce will eventually drive those suppliers away from the domestics. The OEMs justify their actions as necessary in the short run to meet the competition, but, in many ways, they are only asking for the suppliers to pay for their continued inability to change their management model and practices. The domestic industry's major cost problems are an entrenched labor union, increasing pension costs, and rising healthcare burdens for which there are no quick answers. In desperation, they turn to their supply base to reduce current prices as a stop-gap measure. The problem is that as the OEMs lose share, the suppliers see that their own futures lie in working more closely with the foreign manufacturers who more fully embrace the collaborative approach, such as Toyota.

This situation has no easy answer, but many analysts are afraid that the domestic manufacturers are in a death spiral that accelerates with increased use of adversarial behavior. At a time when common sense says they should be building a closer team to jointly fight competition, they are using arbitrary and dictatorial tactics to drive a wedge between their supply base and themselves. American management simply refuses to see the longer outcome and continues to revert to techniques that have failed in the past: asking suppliers to make up for the manufacturer's own faults over the years, which is a suicidal approach. Difficult times do require tougher measures. But those tougher measures do not necessarily mean more adversarial tactics.

A Sign of Hope?

During the third quarter of 2004, it appears that the senior levels of the domestic U.S. automobile manufacturers suddenly recognized the obvious need to change their approach. They have started to make public comments about how their industry should adopt ways to work more closely. In a talk to industry executives reported in the local Detroit newspapers, Dieter Zetsche, CEO of the Chrysler Group of DaimlerChrysler, made what was viewed by many as a startling confession. Zetsche announced; "To say that it's in our mutual (supplier and OEM) interest to find ways to work together is a gross understatement."[2] He went on to admit that the negative tactics used in the industry have taken their toll on both sides. "It's absolutely true that there has been a lot of blood letting recently in this industry," he stated. "Believe me, it hasn't been a pleasant experience."

Those statements indicate that, at least at the top and externally, some auto executives understand the advantages of collaboration and are trying to stop the warfare that exists with their suppliers. But, almost in direct response, at the same meeting the Ford vice president of global purchasing, Tony Brown, showed how ingrained the adversarial approach is within the system by giving this response: "We are individually and collectively tasked for optimizing our bottom line for our respective companies. Our relationship, by design, is set up to have some tension in it." This appears to be more of a caution to the suppliers not to anticipate an invitation from him to work together.

That is precisely the problem. In an adversarial atmosphere that has been poisoned by years of harshly misapplied leverage and mistrust, there is no reason to believe that behavior will change without strong and overt direction. Having used and profited from the Extended Enterprise® in the past, DaimlerChrysler might be able to revert back to its pace-setting cooperative relationships. It is encouraging to see that Chrysler's management still accepts the principles of collaboration even after having taken a step backward by dropping the SCORE program. Could it be that their organization has once again realized that the answer to continued growth and profitability is to join with rather than fight against suppliers? Zetsche's comments are particularly encouraging because he has seen through personal experience how both systems operate. Conversely, Ford apparently has a lot of work to do in convincing its organization to find ways to reduce the "tension" created and to get beyond each party suboptimizing its respective position.

The domestic American suppliers to the auto industry have other alternatives than to wait for the domestic OEMs to heal themselves. They are rapidly moving to embrace the expanded or newly arrived foreign manufacturers that do not operate in the same way that the dying Big Three do. Toyota and Nissan are expanding their U.S. vehicle assembly capacity and are being joined here by the recently successful Koreans from Hyundai and Kia. These companies need a U.S. supply base and are expanding their local sourcing here. The U.S. part suppliers are chasing them with the energy of hounds at a hunt. The foreign auto transplants are offering long-term commitments and jointly developed cost targets that are rewarded with contracts that grow in volume as sales increase. Examples such as the mutual success between Toyota and

Denso or Aisin Seiki show that collaboration can produce a better and more profitable relationship. Although the domestic part makers might have some remaining affinity for the Big Three as customers, it is waning as their adversarial tactics increase.

The more widespread concern is that the situation existing in the Big Three automakers is not unique to that industry. Many of our oldest and most established commercial industries have, or could, follow the same dangerous path as autos. It has already happened in steel, is currently in process in the airline and publishing businesses, and probably will spread to the healthcare industry as it takes more political heat. In doing so, the dislocation of workers, both blue and white collar, will create wrenching changes in our economy and the middle-class way of life that was the basis for our post–World War II economic growth. We can wait for the really bad things to happen, or we can try to change things now while there is still some time to react.

Managed Collaboration Is the Answer

Things are not only bad, but they could become a lot worse if fundamental changes aren't made soon. The answer that has been proposed and outlined here is to adopt a genuine and differentiated collaborative management philosophy. True collaboration must embrace the entire firm, from the CEO down to the lowest-level worker and the union. Opening up jobs that were previously closed and structured will impact everyone. The CEO will have to learn to deal equally with other leaders in supplier firms to create a trusting environment. Line workers will have to accept working shoulder to shoulder with workers from outside firms, some of whom might have different wages and benefits. Collaboration permits companies related in a common enterprise to streamline their mutual operations, reduce overhead costs, and speed up the product-development process. The advantages are that everyone can share in the sustained profitability and security of growth rather than riding the downward spiral of adversarial commerce.

This might sound too good to be true, but it is not. Effective collaboration techniques require active and overt management actions. A change to such actions can't be left to laissez faire, to "goodie two shoes" altruistic styles or people. It needs more up-front planning in addition to the transparent measurement of progress toward clearly defined goals and targets. It is definitely not for the faint-hearted or for managers who like to be on autopilot. Some people will not be able to make the conversion, but the good thing is that, for everyone who fails, there is at least one individual who will find the collaborative approach to be more rewarding and challenging. The transition will not be easy, but it certainly is less onerous than waiting for a pink slip or watching stock prices fall because of the negative results of the command and control adversarial style.

Managed collaboration means that a company is responsible for actively managing and developing its supply chain. It also means that the lower-tiered companies must take the responsibility to manage their own internal supply chains. There must be increased planning and communication between these two activities because they are so interrelated. As the roller lifter example in Chapter 3, "Ending Adversarial Commerce," showed, the complexity of modern supply chains requires more defined roles and intercompany coordination than ever. Each link in the chain needs to understand how it relates to the eventual customer and to the other links. This requires breaking the old mold of isolation and control.

It's Not Just Theory

The concept of managed collaboration is not just theory, but is actually being practiced today by one of the most successful companies, Toyota. Over a period of decades, Toyota has built lasting and trusting relationships with many of its critical suppliers. The company has divided its supply base into noncore companies that provide more standardized commodities and core suppliers that provide complex engineered systems such as transmissions or electronic controls. The noncore companies are dealt with via normal commercial tactics. Those companies that provide the more complicated and expensive parts are cultivated as partners focused on cost reduction and product development.

Toyota works closely with its core partners to define relationships, share information, and integrate that information into their design process. These relationships feature long-term horizons so that investment can be amortized over longer, more secure periods instead of being front-loaded. With these longer-term commitments, suppliers are more willing to coinvest in Toyota's future than under the traditional shorter-term relationships used by domestic suppliers. Admittedly, Toyota often holds a minority share of these core suppliers' equity, such as 25 percent of Denso, or Aisin Seiki up to 40 percent at Toyota Gosei, a seat manufacturer. U.S. car companies have tended to follow a different practice of either owning all of a supplier (by vertically integrating it) or staying completely removed to remain free to shop the business. The strange thing is that, even with equity ownership, Toyota has encouraged suppliers such as Denso to take on business with its direct competitors, such as GM and Ford. Toyota feels so secure in its relationship with Denso that, even with Denso expanding its business with other car companies, Toyota is not threatened. In fact, Toyota enjoys the benefits of volume and profit sharing from money made off its competitors doing business with Denso.

Managed collaboration works and directly helps Toyota stay ahead of its industry. The lessons learned in how it relates to companies such as Denso and Aisin Seiki are models for other companies to follow and proof that collaboration brings strength rather than weakness. Toyota is organized around the concept of cooperation, and it manages the process better than any other company. It seems so simple in its practice that this should have been copied long ago. And that is just what the Chinese and Korean manufacturers are doing while American companies continue to try to refine the old adversarial system.

What Can I Do?

The conversion to collaboration involves major changes at the most senior levels of a firm. Because there can be only one CEO in a company, you might be tempted to think that there need to be only 500 executives involved in implementation in the Fortune 500 company list. In actuality, this can't happen, and it doesn't stop like the proverbial buck at the CEO's desk. Implementation can— and must—involve everyone in management to help institute and implement the conversion process. In fact, if you are not involved, your job is threatened and you might be gone. It is as simple and direct as that.

Each level of management has a different responsibility and role in the process. Clearly, the CEO has to set the example and proper tone at the top of the organization. The CEO's role is to stimulate action, act as a coach and champion, and make sure that the plan is honestly being put into place instead of being merely tolerated with lip service. We pointed out instances in which the top person says the right things to the constituents about encouraging trust and shared responsibility, while at the same time internally supporting the old-line harsh tactics at the lower levels. This charade is obvious to everyone, but is still allowed to be practiced and is more prevalent than not.

Although the CEO has the most important strategic role, the power of collaboration is really witnessed at the lower rungs of the corporate ladder. At these working levels, the benefits are actually brought home. The first line foreman's job can be made easier by knowing that the foreman can have a whole supplier plant working in unison with him. The foreman might not directly realize it, but the smoothed delivery and focused operations of the supplier can help make his daily production goal more achievable and at the right cost level. The midlevel engineering manager is freed from the previous drudgery of doing mundane reporting tasks to working directly with experts at suppliers who bring technology that he would never have been able to capture on his own. These are the types of positions for which mutual collaboration can turn a boring job into an exciting one by broadening responsibility and expanding thinking. Instead of being insulated within a cubicle inside an office, using collaboration to reach out to the extended enterprise opens the door of opportunity to achieve tasks that companies and people cannot do on their own.

This situation is not idealistic. It happens every day in companies that understand how to implement managed collaboration. But there is room for using collaboration at lower levels even if your management has not yet seen the light and begun to endorse change. There is hope even if your company is still set in a traditional culture. The answer is to try to institute change within your own scope of responsibility and authority. Although it is obviously easier with the support of senior management, the absence of that support doesn't mean having to continue to labor under the mind-numbing and demoralizing pressure of command and control.

Few jobs are really completely self-contained within a company, with no contact with the outside world. Lawyers work with outside counsel, accountants face off with independent auditors, skilled tradesmen need supplies from vendors, and maintenance men use independent companies for specialized repairs. The walls of any company are being penetrated at every level in the organization, and that is a good thing that needs to be capitalized upon.

Lower-level managers can still look to the portion of the extended enterprise that affects their own job. They can approach people in the extended enterprise for suggestions, ideas, and proposals to collaborate on projects. Even the most unenlightened managers will respond to well-presented and thought-out proposals that reduce costs. If they don't, they should be fired or you should look for a new job because it is a sign that things might get worse under their leadership.

Making a change toward utilizing an extended enterprise does require analyzing the areas of opportunity and tackling small projects instead of trying for the Big Bang ideas that usually fight entrenched resistance. Often smaller is better and more practical. By working on small ideas that are within your own scope of responsibility, collaboration can be introduced into the firm from the bottom as well as the top. If you think that you can't risk proposing new ideas for fear of rejection or you are completely comfortable working as you currently are, you are not a candidate for being a change agent. There is nothing wrong with that condition, and you can take some solace in knowing that you have at least made it to the step of self-awareness. But do not be surprised when someone else gets promoted past you for imaginative and visionary ideas. That is one old rule that still applies even under collaborative management.

Breaking the Mold: Better Communication

The stranglehold that the adversarial command and control style has on many of our industrial companies can be broken. This approach is a relic of bygone years when workers were uneducated and their jobs were divided into the smallest unit possible for maximum control. In recent times, even such venerable institutions as the U.S. Army have been forced to recognize that better motivation can come by relaxing their previously rigid control structure. Army units now operate as teams, with more enlightened officers letting their highly trained enlisted men take more responsibility. If America's military, one of the oldest bastions of rigid control, can make substantive change in the way it wages warfare, surely America's business firms can do the same on the economic battlefield.

An essential element of making the change is recognizing that more open communication, both within and external to the firm, is a good thing. Misguided overprotection of information is a problem in many companies that feel threatened by outside competition. Actually, hording information is often just a cover for the insecurity that the data might not be as accurate or as useful as it is thought to be. If you don't have to share it, it can't be criticized. That's why companies hold on to unrealistic sales forecasts until it becomes obvious that they are missed, and why stores order way too much inventory even when the buyers know that it will not completely sell out. Sharing the planning information might bring negative challenges or questions from the constituents who are involved. People who don't have to share the information until the last second think they can escape criticism of their plans. In reality, when others realize their mistakes, these people lose their credibility. That's why they use arbitrary demands and ignore common sense, and it is why they give adversarial directions.

We are not talking about building consensus or taking a vote on a recommended action. This is not free-form decision making. All that is being advocated is a managed collaborative approach, to provide useful general details of the decision to the supply base or internal employees instead of keep them in the dark. If they know the plan, they will be more apt to follow it. If the information is kept secret, they will feel isolated and out of the loop. Secret plans build mistrust and create suspicions. Those negative things can build into protectionism and less than enthusiastic participation. People and the companies they work for will hold back in an atmosphere of suspicion.

Improved communication is the heart of opening up a two-way dialogue between parties who are working toward the same goal. Letting everyone involved know that goal is the first step; letting them know the plan is another. You cannot expect an independent company to guess or to assume the objective of its customers if you want to generate collaboration. Certainly, a company will sell its product to almost anyone who will pay for it. But the power of collaboration is to bring more than the specific product to the relationship. It means that ideas, suggestions, and even development expenditures can be forthcoming from suppliers if they know what the client wants and where the client is going. It is an end to just communicating via transactions and moving to a higher level of interrelationship. But it means opening the information flow through a managed process in which only the right amount and right detail of information is provided to the right constituents. If does not mean that everybody needs to know everything or that companies can't retain proprietary information.

There is a spectrum of communication ranging from sharing nothing but an order for a part or service, to completely integrating development and technical planning. It looks simplistically like this:

Spectrum of Intercompany Communication

Transactional	Fully Integrated
Order a part/ send a check	Share planning/joint development

Most companies are more to the left of that spectrum, and only a few make it to the right side of a fully integrated approach. But moving to the right, the exchange of information can only improve relationships and reduce the isolation between important partners. If the firm you run or work for wants to be involved on only the left side and process transactions such as customers shopping in a discount store, collaboration will be difficult for you to implement. The decision to work more closely with others mandates a more open, shared information flow that is still managed by the dominant firm or the one taking on the final assembly or marketing of the completed product or service. You can't work with other people or firms without providing them more information than old-line companies have shared in the past. Improved, more open communication is the heart of a collaborative program.

Breaking the Mold: Taking a Risk

Throughout this book, we have pointed out that it isn't easy to move toward increased collaboration. The present system is very biased against change, and anyone who attempts it runs the risk of being branded as unconventional. However, we are entering unconventional times that require more efficient use of capital, the introduction of conflicting technologies to protect the future, and answers to relocation and training of the entire workforce in many industrial businesses. These challenges could be addressed by using the old-line management structures and styles, but the emergence of aggressive, newly expanding companies from the Far East and Eastern Europe will make it even harder to use the old methods effectively. We cannot afford to meet these challenges by making subtle changes. Tried and true responses to problems might no longer work. In an atmosphere of increasing speed and competition, we must look for other answers.

The tools of collaboration offer the power to help this country's older mature industries revitalize themselves and avoid dropping into eventual decline. No company, regardless of its size, can continue to think that it has absolute and complete control over the numerous other companies that it needs to work with to produce a product or service. There are just too many other alternatives for the related companies to turn to for them to stay with a client that mistreats it with negative adversarial tactics. Sooner or later, the supporting firms will move away from these companies that operate based on distrust and arbitrary control.

There is no guaranteed, foolproof method for a company to break out of the old mold. The concepts we have outlined might appear simple in their form, but they are much more complicated to implement in reality. They have to be adapted, refined, and modified for the unique culture and circumstances in a given firm. We have provided only the elements that must be considered. Management needs to recognize that the current harsh styles of relationship management are failing and that a firm and its managers, workers, suppliers, and dealers must move to a new plane of operation.

The process must be led by managers who want to take a risk and who get excited about making changes. The managers and employees of many companies are incorrectly stereotyped into a single category, but the actuality is that even the most homogenous firm has people who want to try something different and make a difference in their job. These are the people adversarial commerce has held down in their cubicles, doing their job but not contributing to new ideas or changes. These same people are the ones who will leap at the chance to try something that opens up their own scope of responsibility. Stretching people to take new assignments brought more success than failure in the companies we used as examples in this book.

CEOs and senior leaders are important, but we all can't be at that level. Even the recent rapid turnover and the shortening tenure of the CEOs won't permit most of us to reach that position of influence and power. That might be an advantage because: This level tends to be the most conservative of all because CEOs look to their peers for reinforcement and example. It could be that the revolution of collaboration will be mostly led by the middle managers who are just fed up with treating people in adversarial ways and who see the costs it creates and the advantages that a new manner can bring.

One legitimate fear is that, collectively, the management of most American firms does not have the fortitude and strength to break out of the current well-used mold. We are all comfortable following the traditional path. The problem is that the path is leading our companies, our employees, and our country in the wrong direction. Whatever the rest of the world's industrial firms feel about the political and foreign policy of the United States, they look to our economy as the strongest and most established market for them to approach. Foreign firms have the advantage of looking at the way U.S. firms operate and then adopting and modifying their approach as they enter this country seeking new revenue opportunities. Older, mature domestic firms must find new ways to counter these new entries to our traditional markets. That will mean changing the way we manage and deal with the extended enterprise web of companies that are necessary for any firm to conduct business in a modern economy. American managers must rise to the occasion to make changes now, while they can appropriately plan and time the implementation, instead of waiting for the inevitable decline.

Collaborative management requires planning and effort, but it represents a way to capture the power of working as a true team instead of the waste involved in independent isolation of companies on different agendas. It can also make the act of management more exciting and rewarding by introducing some human relations elements into a closed structure. Our economy has not yet had to prove that it can make a transition in which new, smaller high-technology firms will replace older, mature firms who employ so many workers and support even more retirees. Instead of letting nature run its course, managers who embrace collaborative management can help save their firm, their job, and, in likelihood, their economy. There seems to be some risk, but there's much more to gain if we can just break the mold of tradition that drives conformity in our business world.

Endnotes

1. Morgan Stanley Research Report, "India and China: A Special Economic Analysis" 26 July, 2004.

2. Author, Jewel Gopwani, "Car Companies Urged to Improve Relations," *Detroit Free Press* 2 September 2004: pp 1F.

SCORE!

A BETTER WAY TO DO BUSINE$$: MOVING FROM CONFLICT TO COLLABORATION

Supporting Figures and Attachments

Appendix A.1—SCORE Logo

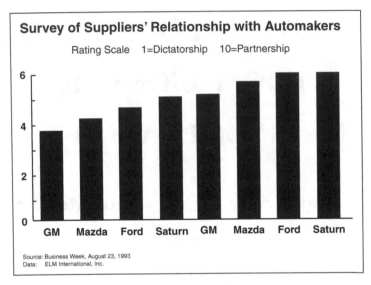

Appendix A.2—Survey of Supplier Relationships

"The following three figures are from a Chrysler supplier meeting presentation," details the types of items suppliers could use to count toward their SCORE objectives.

Ways to SCORE

SCORE Enablers

√ | *Design*
√ | *Process Improvement*
√ | *Materials*
√ | *New Technologies*
√ | *Volume Efficiencies*
√ | *Packaging & Returnable Containers*
√ | *Weight Reduction ($1/lb.)*

SCORE
Supplier COst Reduction Effort

Ways to SCORE

SCORE Enablers

√ | *Content*
√ | *Payment Terms*
√ | *Warranty Reduction*
√ | *Inventory Reduction*
√ | *Complexity Reduction ($20,000/part eliminated)*
√ | *Tier II Sourcing*
√ | *Optimization of Manufacturing Location*

SCORE
Supplier COst Reduction Effort

Ways to SCORE

SCORE Enablers

√ | *Freight/FOB Changes*
√ | *Eliminate Multiple Sourcing*
√ | *Optimization of Validation Requirements*
√ | *Tooling Savings*
√ | *Service Parts*
√ | *Communication*
√ | *Chrysler/Supplier Business Practices*

SCORE
Supplier COst Reduction Effort

Appendix A.3.1-A.3.3—Ways to SCORE

The Extended Enterprise®

What it is

A Chrysler-coordinated process that unifies and extends the business relationships of suppliers and supplier tiers to maximize the effectiveness of vehicle development, minimize total systems costs, and improve quality and customer acceptance.

Appendix A.4—Definition of Extended Enterprise®

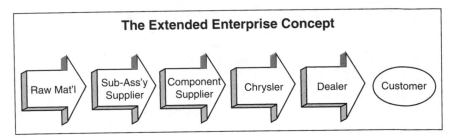

Appendix A.5—Graphic of Extended Enterprise

Appendix A.6 is another stylized graphic showing complicity of supply chain.

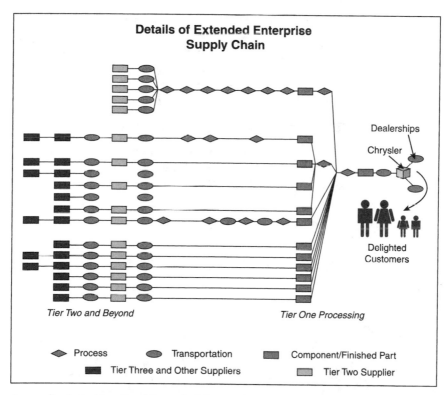

Appendix A.6—Details of Extended Enterprise®

Appendix A.7 is another example of supply chain mapping similar to the Roller Lifter in Chapter 3.

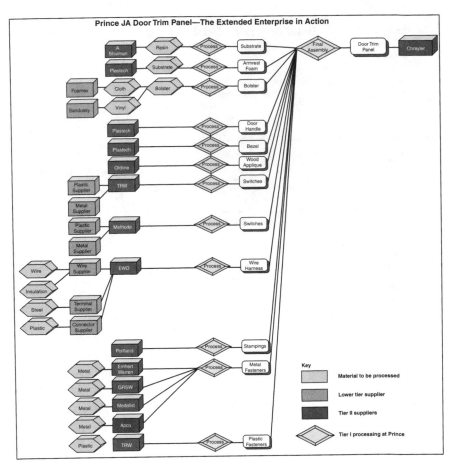

Appendix A.7—Prince JA Door Trim Panel

FOR IMMEDIATE RELEASE

Poor Relationships Costing US Automakers

US Supliers Shifting Support, R&D and Investment to Japanese Automakers, says Annual Benchmark Study

BIRMINGHAM, Mich. July 30—Findings of the annual OEM-Tier 1 Supplier Working Relations Study of automakers' relations with their suppliers suggest more trouble for US automakers' if they don't change the way they deal with their suppliers: The study shows that US suppliers are shifting their loyalties—and resources—to their Japanese customers at the expense of the domestic Big Three.

This trend began to show up in last year's study, but is picking up speed this year as US automakers continue hammering their suppliers for price reductions and multi-million dollar cash givebacks and suppliers are responding by giving them less support.

It is important to note, however, that this shift in loyalty is not driven by cost reduction pressures on suppliers, says the study's author, but rather on how the US automakers work with their suppliers across a wide range of business practices.

"The study shows, again this year, that the US automakers' primary orientation is toward cost reduction, they have little regard for their suppliers, they communicate very poorly and they generally treat suppliers as adversaries rather than trusted partners. In all the other industries we've studied such as aerospace, electronics, and computers, no one treats their suppliers as poorly as the US automakers do." said John W. Henke, Jr., Ph.D., whose firm, Planning Perspectives, Inc. conducts the annual study.

As a result of their respective handling of suppliers, there are some profound shifts going on in the industry that can't help but impact the US Big Three's ability to compete going forward, said Henke. These changes are summarized in the following points:

- Chrysler Ford and GM supplier working relations are failing behind Honda and Toyota at an increasing rate
- Suppliers are shifting resources (capital and R&D expenditures, service and support) to Japanese Big Three, while reducing these for Domestic Big Three
- Suppliers are increasing product quality at a greater rate for the Japanese, while merely maintaining quality levels for US automakers
- Supplier trust of Ford and General Motors has never been lower: conversely, trust for the Japanese OEMs has never been higher

Appendix A.8.1—PPI Press Release 7/30/04

The study shows that the domestic Big Three and Japanese Big Three have fundamentally different approaches to working with their suppliers and suggests that this difference might well be a major factor in the consistently high quality and competitive gains by the Japanese.

In fact, according to the study, in the five key areas measured—Relationship, communication, Help, Hindrance, and Profit Opportunity—the US automakers are 180 degrees opposite their Japanese counterparts. (See Table 1)

TABLE 1		
Criteria	**US Big Three**	**Japanese Big Three**
Project confidential info	Little regard for suppliers' proprietary information or intellectual property	High regard
Open, honest communication	Indifferent, late	High level, timely
Importance of cost vs. quality & technology	Primary focus is on cost	Seek low cost, but balance with quality and technology
Supplier survival	Little regard	Concern for long-term success
Relationship orientation	Adverarial; focus is on OEMs short-term gain	Strategically integrate suppliers into partnership-like relations

It is also why US suppliers continue to prefer doing business with the Japanese, and in some cases would like to drop the US automakers if they could, according to the study.

The overall results of the annual study and the actions listed above are summarized by an annual ranking called the OEM-Supplier Working Relations index (WRI).

The 2004 WRI shows the Japanese automakers continue to move up the scale toward even better relations with their suppliers, while the US automakers remain static at the bottom. Again in 2004, the index shows Toyota and Honda far ahead and ranked at 399 and 384 and respectively, while GM and Ford are at the bottom with a ranking of 144 and 160 (see Table 2). Nissan was ranked 294, and Chrysler was 183.

The 2004 WRI shows that each of the Japanese Big Three significantly improved their positions over 2003 and are well above the industry mean, while Ford and GM are below the industry mean and losing ground. Chrysler was also below the industry mean but improved slightly.

"It's important to note as well that the industry mean rose 16.6% over the three-year period driven by gains made by the Japanese Big Three." said Henke. "In other words, the Japanese OEMs keep raising the bar in the area of supplier working relations and are increasing the gap between themselves and the domestic Big Three.

"What is apparent is that the Japanese OEMs are applying continuous improvement practices to their supplier working relations just as they have done to their manufacturing processes, and as a result they continue to win the cost-quality-technology race."

Appendix A.8.2—PPI Press Release 7/30/04

Table 2. Overall OEM—Supplier Working Relation Index for 2002—2004

OEM	YEAR			2003-2004 % Change	2002-2004 % Change
	2002	2003	2004		
Toyota	314	334	399	19.5%	27.1%
Honda	297	316	384	21.5%	29.3%
Nissan	227	259	294	13.5%	29.5%
Industry Mean	224	234	261	11.5%	16.6%
Chrysler	175	177	183	3.4%	4.6%
Ford	167	161	160	−0.6%	−4.2%
GM	161	156	144	−7.8%	−10.6%

The 2004 study involved analyzing OEM-supplier relations across 852 buying situations and ranked the OEMs in five areas that comprise 17 variables. Based on this analysis, the WRI for 2004 did not change for the domestic OEMs, but improved for each of the Japanese Big Three. Notably, the price reduction demands an OEM makes on suppliers has zero impact on the WRI. Rather, it is the *total* working environment of the OEM that impacts the WRI.

"It's clear from comparing our 2002 and 2003 studies with 2004, that the domestic OEMs have done virtually nothing to change their working relations with suppliers over the past four years, while the Japanese Big Three continue to improve. Both groups are seeing the results of their respective actions," sazid Henke.

"The domestic OEMs ahve assumed that getting price reductions from their suppliers and having good supplier working relations are mutually exclusive. Nothing could be further from the truth. Honda, Toyota and Nissan, recognize that they can pressure their suppliers for considerable price reductions and quality improvements and still have good supplier working relations. It all comes down to how you work with people that determines whether or not you get the bets performance from them."

The results of the survey also indicate why OEMs with good supplier working relations gain a competitive advantage. "Over the years, we have seen a consistent pattern that shows OEM working relations directly affects supplier behavior. Our studies show that the further up the index an OEM moves, the more suppliers are willing to help the OEM. Suppliers will share more technology with the OEM, are more willing to invest in new technology in anticipation of new business, and will provide higher quality goods and higher levels of service to the OEM. The Japanese OEMs clearly understand this and it's helping them gain competitive advantage and market share," he said.

Appendix A.8.3—PPI Press Release 7/30/04

> The 2004 supplier survey was conducted in July. This year, it involved responses from 223 Tier 1 suppliers including 36 of the Top 50 and was based on 852 buying situations. The participating suppliers' combined sales represent 48% of the OEM's annual purchase of components.
>
> **About PPI**
> Since 1990, PPI has specialized in developing and implementing in-depth surveys of suppliers for the automotive OEMs and Tier 1 suppliers. In 2001, PPI initiated its syndicated Annual North American Automotive Tier 1 Supplier Study. These studies have become benchmarks for the industry and provide critical sales and financial planning information for suppliers and their sales, marketing, and financial staffs, as well as a means by which OEMs and their purchasing staffs can get a reality check on their working relationships with suppliers. PPI is based in Birmingham, Michigan and can be reached at +01.248.644.7690.

Appendix A.8.4—PPI Press Release 7/30/04

Appendix A.9.1–A.9.3 contain details of a 1996 independent survey showing how Chrysler compared to other OEMs. The Extended Enterprise® improved important areas over domestic competition.

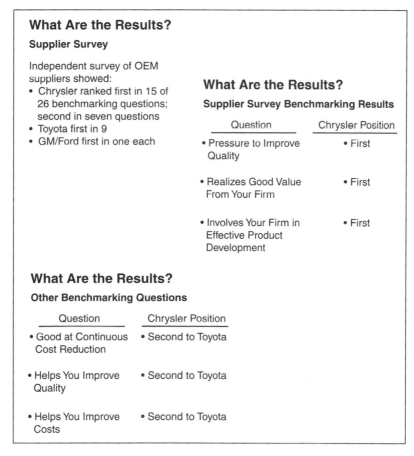

What Are the Results?

Supplier Survey

Independent survey of OEM suppliers showed:
- Chrysler ranked first in 15 of 26 benchmarking questions; second in seven questions
- Toyota first in 9
- GM/Ford first in one each

What Are the Results?

Supplier Survey Benchmarking Results

Question	Chrysler Position
• Pressure to Improve Quality	• First
• Realizes Good Value From Your Firm	• First
• Involves Your Firm in Effective Product Development	• First

What Are the Results?

Other Benchmarking Questions

Question	Chrysler Position
• Good at Continuous Cost Reduction	• Second to Toyota
• Helps You Improve Quality	• Second to Toyota
• Helps You Improve Costs	• Second to Toyota

Appendix A.9.1-A.9.3—Supplier Survey Results

INDEX

"Great schools have…endeavored to do more than keep up to the respectable standard of a recent past; they have labored to supply the needs of an advancing and exacting world…"

— **Joseph Wharton,** *Entrepreneur and Founder of the Wharton School*

The Wharton School is recognized around the world for its innovative leadership and broad academic strengths across every major discipline and at every level of business education. It is one of four undergraduate and 12 graduate and professional schools of the University of Pennsylvania. Founded in 1881 as the nation's first collegiate business school, Wharton is dedicated to creating the highest value and impact on the practice of business and management worldwide through intellectual leadership and innovation in teaching, research, publishing and service.

Wharton's tradition of innovation includes many firsts—the first business textbooks, the first research center, the MBA in health care management—and continues to innovate with new programs, new learning approaches, and new initiatives. Today Wharton is an interconnected community of students, faculty, and alumni who are shaping global business education, practice, and policy.

Wharton is located in the center of the University of Pennsylvania (Penn) in Philadelphia, the fifth-largest city in the United States. Students and faculty enjoy some of the world's most technologically advanced academic facilities. In the midst of Penn's tree-lined, 269-acre urban campus, Wharton students have access to the full resources of an Ivy League university, including libraries, museums, galleries, athletic facilities, and performance halls. In recent years, Wharton has expanded access to its management education with the addition of Wharton West, a San Francisco academic center, and The Alliance with INSEAD in France, creating a global network.

Making Strategy Work
Leading Effective Execution and Change
BY LAWRENCE G. HREBINIAK

Without effective execution, no business strategy can succeed. Unfortunately, most managers know far more about developing strategy than about executing it—and overcoming the difficult political and organizational obstacles that stand in their way. In this book, Wharton professor Lawrence Hrebiniak offers the first comprehensive, disciplined process model for making strategy work in the real world. Drawing on his unsurpassed experience, Hrebiniak shows why execution is even more important than many senior executives realize, and sheds powerful new light on why businesses fail to deliver on even their most promising strategies. Next, he offers a systematic roadmap for execution that encompasses every key success factor: organizational structure, coordination, information sharing, incentives, controls, change management, culture, and the role of power and influence in your business.

ISBN 013146745X, © 2005, 408 pp., $27.95

Capitalism at the Crossroads
The Unlimited Business Opportunities in Solving the World's Most Difficult Problems
BY STUART L. HART

Capitalism is indeed at a crossroads, facing international terrorism, worldwide environmental change, and an accelerating backlash against globalization. Your company is at a crossroads, too: finding new strategies for profitable growth is now more challenging than it has ever been. Both sets of problems are intimately linked. In this book you'll learn how to identify sustainable products and technologies that can drive new growth while also helping to solve today's most crucial social and environmental problems. Drawing on his experience consulting with leading companies and NGOs worldwide, Hart shows how to become truly indigenous to all your markets—and avoid the pitfalls of traditional "greening" and "sustainability" strategies. This book doesn't just point the way to a capitalism that is more inclusive and more welcome: it offers specific techniques you can use to recharge innovation, growth, and profitability in your enterprise.

ISBN 0131439871, © 2005, 288 pp., $27.95